THE PRIMARY HEADTEACHER'S

handbook

THE PRIMARY
HEADTEACHER'S

the essential guide for primary heads   **handbook**

ROGER SMITH

KOGAN
PAGE

First published in 2002

Kogan Page Limited
120 Pentonville Road
London N1 9JN
UK

Stylus Publishing Inc
22883 Quicksilver Drive
Sterling VA 20166-2012
USA

The views expressed in this book are those of the author and are not necessarily the same as those of *The Times Educational Supplement*.

British Library Cataloguing in Publication Data

A CIP record for this book is available from the British Library.

ISBN 0 7494 3537 2

Typeset by JS Typesetting, Wellingborough, Northants
Printed and bound in Great Britain by Clays Ltd, St Ives plc

CONTENTS

INTRODUCTION

It has never been easy to define what headteachers actually do but whatever it is, they need to be able to do it successfully and avoid the traumas and doubts that Toulouse Lautrec must have felt when asked how good he was at basketball. Now that those in positions of leadership in schools are subject to growing public scrutiny, it is important that they demonstrate that their schools are skilfully and successfully led and managed. In working towards success and effectiveness, the headteacher as school leader will, in effect, be providing staff with access to and support from senior management through regular discussions, periods outside their classrooms to reflect upon practice and opportunities to develop their roles as coordinators. In other words, they will recognise that the need to lead lies alongside the need to develop the skills of all other colleagues.

Effective headteachers are able to approach positively and deal competently with the enormous changes that are taking place. At the same time they will have inspired committed attitudes in their teachers by creating organisational structures which make even the most ordinary teacher capable of extraordinary achievements.

The leadership role of the headteacher is vital in raising standards and if we were to suggest what the qualities of a good, well-led and well-managed primary school were, we would list some or all of the following:

❑ The headteacher has to understand the needs of the school and be actively involved in the school's work without exercising total control over the rest of the staff.
❑ They are involved in all curriculum discussions and decisions and influence the content of curriculum guidelines without undermining the authority of curriculum coordinators.
❑ They monitor teaching and influence teaching strategies.
❑ They involve the deputy head and senior teachers in decision making.
❑ They feel confident that teachers are doing their job and don't feel the need to intervene constantly.
❑ Staff development and training are high priorities.

1

❑ There is a balanced curriculum with appropriate emphasis placed on core subjects.

❑ Classrooms are orderly with an emphasis on teaching, learning and assessment.

❑ The headteacher involves governors in strategic debate about the school's present and future.

❑ Parents are consulted at appropriate times in the school year.

❑ He or she is considerate towards staff and maintains an ethos and culture that is inclusive of staff, children and parents.

❑ The headteacher makes sure that there is an agreed and effective school development plan with a sense of direction that anticipates future developments.

❑ He or she is an effective communicator of the school's successes and presents a positive image of the school, staff and children.

It is possible to go on and produce a longer list but doing this would not create a definition that is easier to understand, but only one that has more sections and is even more complex. It should be obvious that there is a need for strong purposeful leadership together with other factors such as delegating and sharing responsibilities and tasks, together with managing the existing continuity as well as the frequent changes that take place. Good headteachers have to be able to manage and lead in such a way that the separate parts of the jigsaw fit together to meet the needs of teachers, children and parents and at the same time satisfy the standards set by those who hold the school accountable, such as Ofsted inspectors. Leadership is a keyword that will be used over and over again but it is an elusive concept without any clear definition. There are, however, subtle differences between managing the school and leading it. Table 0.1 attempts to draw some distinctions which will have a bearing on many of the chapters in this book.

Table 0.1 *Management and leadership*

MANAGEMENT	LEADERSHIP
Solve problems	Manage problem solving
Achieve immediate results	Have a long-term vision
Maintain the status quo	Change and develop the status quo
Develop structures and processes	Involve people
Maintain the existing culture and climate	Develop new cultures and climates
Delegate	Coach and empower people
Plan, organise and control	Have a grand design and purpose
Hold power from the position of head	Hold power by building relationships

Raising standards requires effective management and sound educational leadership which, working together, will avoid a negative ethos which results in a lack of any sense of community where children and staff feel undervalued and where there are low standards, lethargy and apathy.

One important factor in being a successful head is to know how each individual fits into the organisation and how they relate to each other. It is not enough for an effective head just to know how. I am sure that the Venus de Milo knew how to play a piano accordion but was dramatically incapable of doing so. Headteachers have to be able to 'act' and 'do' in order to achieve the results that they want and are capable of. In the early 1990s, the importance of school management was beginning to be taken seriously. *Developing School Management: The Way Forward* (HMSO, 1990) suggested that the headteacher's leadership is important for three basic reasons:

❑ to improve the learning of all pupils;
❑ to develop, understand and monitor individuals, teams and the whole institution;
❑ to develop the school's capacity to understand itself and evaluate its own performance.

These are all excellent reasons for improving the standards of management and leadership and this book has been written to help headteachers rise to the many challenges facing them and to manage effectively everything that happens in the busy primary school. It has also been written to encourage deputies, senior teachers and teachers to aspire to become headteachers and to inspire governors and teacher trainers to understand more clearly how an effective headteacher will be able to create and sustain a successful school.

The chapters are as follows:

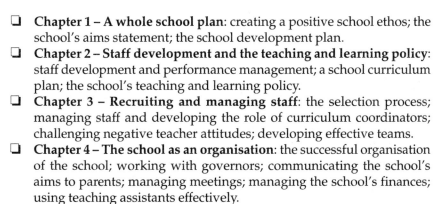

❑ **Chapter 1 – A whole school plan**: creating a positive school ethos; the school's aims statement; the school development plan.
❑ **Chapter 2 – Staff development and the teaching and learning policy**: staff development and performance management; a school curriculum plan; the school's teaching and learning policy.
❑ **Chapter 3 – Recruiting and managing staff**: the selection process; managing staff and developing the role of curriculum coordinators; challenging negative teacher attitudes; developing effective teams.
❑ **Chapter 4 – The school as an organisation**: the successful organisation of the school; working with governors; communicating the school's aims to parents; managing meetings; managing the school's finances; using teaching assistants effectively.

❏ **Chapter 5 – Three problem areas**: stress management; time management; the management of conflict.

❏ **Chapter 6 – Leadership**: Leadership skills; what is successful leadership; managing change; accountability.

❏ **Chapter 7 – Managing successful teachers and effective teaching**: developing effective teaching; successful classroom management; dealing with disaffected children; assertive teaching; behaviour management; raising standards through target setting and assessment.

❏ **Chapter 8 – Developing curriculum managers and curriculum policies**: the role of curriculum coordinators; planning the curriculum; differentiation; homework; sharing the curriculum with parents.

❏ **Chapter 9 – Managing a successful inspection**: a pre-Ofsted audit; analysing the school's strengths; the inspection process; selling your school as a successful organisation.

A WHOLE SCHOOL PLAN

Most effective headteachers are good at thinking strategically. In other words, they have a broad vision of where the school is and where they want it to be. At the same time, they are constantly developing ideas, absorbing information from colleagues within the school and from outside which influences how they plan to make improvements. They are able to focus on the 'big picture' and set challenging goals to help them get where they want to go. During this process, they need to create a positive ethos and this is the starting point, because without it heads and teachers can work, innovate and manage change until they drop, and the school will still be much less effective than it should be. Schools, and the structures and organisations within them, need to be able to develop attitudes that will not only help pupils learn but will show them how to do it and how to continue to want to learn.

CREATING AN APPROPRIATE SCHOOL ETHOS

Schools have their own feelings and vibrations that make each one unique and it is this ethos or culture that can determine whether some schools are more effective than others. There are many indicators of a positive ethos and they include the following:

- ❏ Pupils are happy.
- ❏ Pupils work hard.
- ❏ Pupils are treated fairly.
- ❏ Bullying is a rare occurrence.
- ❏ Pupils receive help when they need it.
- ❏ There is a lively creative atmosphere that is conducive to learning.
- ❏ Teachers motivate their classes.
- ❏ Discipline is positive and consistent.
- ❏ All those working in the school and visiting it are made to feel welcome.

The more effective the school is in promoting these attitudes and 'selling' its successes to all interested parties, the more positive will be its ethos in the eyes of all those who are able to promote its interests. Headteachers, however, will need to have clear views about what makes a successful ethos and why certain factors within the climate and structure of the school make it effective in preparing its pupils for the future.

It has long been accepted that, while schools cannot wholly eliminate the effects of social differences between pupils, they can, through their own good practice, improve the standards of work, behaviour and attitudes of all pupils. There is now a fairly standard list of what headteachers need to be able to do in order to create a positive ethos. Table 1.1 is a list of factors which, if they are to be influential, have to be 'sold' to parents, governors, teachers and pupils. Many of the factors in Table 1.1 will form part of other chapters.

Table 1.1 *Factors that create a positive ethos*

❏ Effective and powerful leadership.

❏ Senior teachers who are involved in decision making.

❏ All teachers need to be consulted and feel that they own and are part of decisions that directly affect them.

❏ There needs to be consistency and continuity throughout the school, eg in terms of discipline patterns, homework policies, teaching strategies, resource management, timetable structures etc.

❏ Teaching needs to be structured, matched to pupils' needs, well paced and lively.

❏ All teaching should be intellectually challenging for all pupils.

❏ The environment of the school will be task and work orientated, ie every pupil will recognise that learning is the norm rather than the exception.

❏ There will be lots of communication between teachers and pupils both inside and outside the classroom.

❏ Record keeping and assessment are sensible and thorough and are communicated to parents when necessary in a way that can be understood.

❏ There is a positive climate where emphasis is placed on praise rather than criticism.

❏ Control in classrooms is firm, fair and consistent, with children being treated as individuals.

❏ Activities are organised to take place outside the classroom as a means of offering pupils wider experience and a way of putting the academic content of the curriculum into a different context.

Selling the ethos

In making sure that everyone who is a stakeholder in the school is aware of the basic ideals that make up the whole school ethos, it is important to communicate regularly with them. The school prospectus should take the lead in this, but newsletters, meetings with parents, open evenings with a specific theme, such as numeracy, for example, together with school policies will all have a part to play.

The communication structures within the school need to be accessible to all teachers. Meetings, discussion groups, working parties etc should all reinforce the positive ethos. Governors and the community should be approached through language that is jargon-free and non-patronising. As many subcommittees as possible should involve parents, governors and teachers working together. In many ways, selling the ethos is about marketing basic ideas about what needs to happen for the school to be successful.

Powerful leadership

The concept of leadership will be examined in more detail later in the book and it features in both the Introduction and the Conclusion. It is important, however, to examine some basic concepts, because the success of any positive whole school ethos will fall by the wayside without strong and knowledgeable leadership. Leadership style matters in that it can make or break any positive image that the school tries to create. In its simplest form, there is a continuum that stretches from a permissive leadership style at one extreme to an autocratic leadership style at the other. If the style is permissive then the school will tend to be a collection of individuals in separate classrooms, with little in common and no corporate sense of school ethos. In other words, everyone may well be working hard, but they will be doing so on their own, with little or no corporate guidance. On the other hand, the autocratic style can be equally ineffective in how it creates image and ethos. Decisions will be taken without consultation and there will be a similar lack of collective responsibility about what the school stands for. What is needed is a compromise between autocratic and permissive leadership that will raise standards as well as maintain good relationships.

Positive and negative aspects of whole school ethos

The 1989 Elton Report, *Discipline in Schools*, suggests that schools where there is little evidence of a positive ethos suffer more from poor behaviour, graffiti and litter. The negative aspects of such schools include a failure to achieve a sense of community, failure to make staff and pupils feel valued, and a tendency to expect poor behaviour and standards. The report sees a definite link between effectiveness, positive ethos and good management by the headteacher. It recognises that there needs to be a positive commitment to change by the head and senior teachers and that this commitment needs to be shared by other staff and governors.

Negative aspects could be improved by the following actions:

❑ Set up working parties involving teachers, ancillary staff and teaching assistants. Give these groups positive working briefs, eg how do we improve behaviour at lunchtime?
❑ Involve children and parents, using questionnaires and discussion groups.
❑ Bring the community into the school by letting the premises during the evening to as many groups as possible. Ask the community for suggestions about what they want from school – adult learning, sports etc.
❑ Bring community leaders in to talk to classes.
❑ Make open evenings more accessible and varied.
❑ Tell parents what you are doing and ask for their advice.
❑ Set up policy-forming groups which create policies such as behaviour and discipline.
❑ Use assemblies and lessons to put forward a more positive image and indicate to all children, by praising rather than criticising, that their contributions are valued.

What happens in classrooms

Of course, what is taught and how classrooms are managed influences how parents and pupils see the ethos and culture of the school. These are key issues in any debate about ethos.

What happens in classrooms is to a large extent governed by the skills and attitudes of individual teachers but they are affected and influenced by the style of leadership offered by the headteacher. There should be an informed debate about teaching methods and parents should understand that what happens in classrooms is work orientated and largely about making sure that all children achieve their maximum potential. The school needs to communicate its search for raised standards and excellence through newsletters and meetings. The Elton Report suggests that positive educational processes (and it is these that will raise standards) are organised more successfully by those teachers who have good group management skills. This has implications for the selection of staff, performance management and the school's policy on staff development. Schools who want to create and maintain a positive ethos need to make sure that all teachers have the appropriate skills and training. Table 1.2 lists some of the skills that are needed if teachers are to be effective. It is not a definitive list and this is a subject for discussion in a later chapter.

Table 1.2 *Some effective teaching skills*

Good teachers are usually able to do the following:

❑ Relate easily to their pupils.
❑ Hold pupils' attention.
❑ Have the ability to model the kind of behaviour that they expect from pupils, eg if they expect courtesy, they are courteous.
❑ In controlling pupils, use the appropriate body language and styles that are necessary, eg alter posture, tone of voice etc when angry or when praising children.
❑ Reflect on their own practice and analyse their own successes and faults.
❑ Use praise in the classroom far more than criticism.
❑ Plan in the long, medium and short term so that lesson content is appropriate to various levels of ability.
❑ Ensure that what they teach and how they teach is matched to pupils' ability.

It is important to bear in mind that both parents and children will know who they perceive to be an effective teacher and who isn't. A believable, secure and positive ethos will depend on teaching quality and how this quality is recognised. In recruiting staff and retaining those who are already working in school, it is essential to recognise their worth and to continue to motivate and develop their strengths. A charter mark such as Investors in People will provide an excellent framework, but this kind of staffing structure will only work if headteachers and senior managers create an environment where the individual teacher can thrive within a team which is working together to achieve success for everyone. Such teams need to be aware of the following areas.

Pupil needs

All pupils need to achieve success and, at the same time, no children need to fail. Special Educational Needs (SEN) policies are essential and they need to be backed by appropriate resources, which will include support teachers and teaching assistants. There needs to be a commitment to inclusion and a will to create opportunities for learning to be successful. There need to be strategies for differentiating within the classroom for all ability levels as well as a whole school policy for those children who are gifted and talented.

Assessment and recording

More and more assessment is now the norm and the pattern in most schools is:

❑ baseline assessment in the Reception (Foundation) class;
❑ assessments such as COPs to identify early language needs in Year 1;
❑ national tests at 7 in Year 2;
❑ QCA and possibly NFER tests in Years 3–5;
❑ national tests in Year 6.

It is important that parents and pupils understand the processes involved in assessment and are not persuaded that national test results and league tables are fully representative of the school's achievements. There has to be evidence of attainment that parents can understand. It will be a positive achievement for schools if they are able to hold open evenings where parents can see lots of pupils' work, listen to supportive talks and discuss on an individual basis their child's achievements. The school's record-keeping processes will have to be effective for this to take place smoothly. By assessing and reporting in this way, schools should have a profile on each pupil that will help both teachers and parents understand the level of attainment and progress of each child.

Forward planning

Teachers as well as headteachers need to 'own' what is happening in their schools. They need to play a part in development planning and in the production and implementation of the School Development Plan. By doing this, they will have a vested interest in creating and maintaining all the positive initiatives that are generated by all the plans to improve what is happening in the school. Planning meetings must be relevant, well chaired and with a set agenda. They must allow effective debate and be committed to taking and acting on decisions.

Resources

Resources are the tools of teaching and everyone must be involved in acquiring and sharing them. There are implications for staffing, because teachers and teaching assistants are the most important resources for raising standards and maintaining an effective working atmosphere and a positive ethos. Human resources need to work where they are needed and with children whom they can teach successfully. Individuals and small groups with similar needs should be targeted so that at the beginning of each year teaching assistants are deployed efficiently. If there are teachers who are non-class based, they should be used to meet the demands of the School Development Plan. For example, if one of the sections refers to raising standards in writing in Key Stage 1, teachers and teaching assistants should be available to work with children who need to improve their writing.

School PTAs should also be part of the discussion that decides what the school needs. They will be more likely to provide 'luxury' items such as outside play equipment, video cameras etc. There are also moves in some schools to attract outside sponsorship through links with local industry. When this happens, it is often possible to receive large sums of money for specific projects such as new libraries which have an obvious and lasting effect on the school and which cannot fail to improve the sense of well-being among staff and children.

Communication

It is important that everyone who works in school knows what is happening. If there are teachers or teaching assistants who feel that there is something that everyone knows and they don't, they are likely to be disgruntled. But, it is also true that if the aim is for teachers to be consistent when they are interpreting whole school policies, eg on behaviour, then it is important that all teachers and teaching assistants actually know what the policy is. Parents also need to know what is happening, and lively and regular newsletters will help. If there are parents where English is a second language, these newsletters need to be translated. This will ensure that no group of parents will feel isolated from what is happening in school.

Within the school, pigeon holes, staffroom whiteboards, staffroom diaries, and Monday morning business meetings giving details of the week ahead will all help to keep everyone as well informed as possible. One common problem with communication is that everyone blames other people or the system if they don't happen to have the same information as everyone else. They need to be reminded that communication is a two-way process and, for example, it is no good having a staffroom diary if teachers don't read it; similarly, pigeon holes only work if they are emptied regularly.

Personal development

If teachers and teaching assistants are the most expensive resource, they are also the most useful. Without their support and their effectiveness, the school will not have a positive ethos that attracts parents and children and raises standards. They have to be trained and staff development should be a natural and important aspect of how the school works. Staff development and training has to be matched to the school's needs and these will already have been recognised in the School Development Plan and through performance management reviews. The School Development Plan will not work effectively if training is not available. Similarly, if teachers have identified their own performance management target, they need training if they are expected to meet that target. Using the school's own expertise in staff development as well as that of outside agencies will promote a positive feeling of growth and development. Records need to be kept of all training so that governors can be kept informed. If they and the parents are told that staff development is a high priority then their perceptions of the school's expertise will be enhanced.

General administration

Regular routines have to be established. Schools are about the quality of teaching and learning and how this raises standards. An effective administration will ensure that teachers are not expected to handle too many administrative tasks. This will mean that school administrators or secretaries or bursars have an important role to play in creating a positive ethos. They are also the first point of contact for parents and visitors, so they must have the kind of attitudes and personalities that show efficiency, friendliness, organisational ability etc. They also need training. This means that staff development needs to be seen as a whole school concept that applies equally to administration and other non-teaching staff.

A style of working

Perhaps the next stage is to try to define a style of working that will help develop a positive ethos within the boundaries of all the areas already suggested. Table 1.3 identifies four attributes that together will build up a specific style.

Table 1.3 *Style attributes*

1. Vision	Good schools will be aware of what is happening nationally and locally and their success in their own eyes and of the community will be seen in the vision they project, which avoids parochialism and absorbs all that is best in current educational thinking.
2. Foresight	Schools have their own 'feelings' and 'attitudes' that set them apart and make them unique. The more positive they feel about what they are doing, the easier it is to think ahead and absorb changes into how they work and how the individual, the school and the community interact.
3. Faith	Everyone needs to have faith in their colleagues' professionalism and to recognise that the whole school is a team that is working to meet the learning needs of all the children in the school of whatever ability.
4. Imagination	Schools with a clearly defined, well-respected and positive ethos have a corporate excitement about moving forward and by doing this well, they reduce anxiety, minimise stress and refuse to be complacent.

Two main issues need to be considered as a result of the four style attributes in Table 1.3:

1. **Change** – This is about moving forward and improving the quality of teaching and learning. It can involve such simple things as refurbishing the entrance hall by creating a space for displays and furniture to sit on, or providing more litter bins to reduce the amount of litter that is dropped. It is also about making changes to difficult perennial problems such as the school's stance on bullying, racism or gender issues.
2. **Capable people** – To be able to make such changes the headteacher will have had to surround her or himself with capable people who are

full of positive ideas, are approachable, easy to contact and not trapped behind closed doors. They will not be easily threatened and will feel valued enough to have strong views about what is right for the school.

Avoiding being negative

A school that has this tenuous thing called a positive ethos will be able to avoid being defensive and negative about what it is trying to do. They will be able to use all the marketing and media tools at their disposal to shout out their successes and celebrate their achievements. There are simplistic performance indicators which at one level are able to chart a school's effectiveness. They include:

❑ absence rates, especially those that are unauthorised;
❑ average attendance over a year;
❑ test results, eg the percentage of children reaching level 2 at age 7 and the percentage reaching level 4 at age 11, although another indicator which might suggest success is the percentage of children reaching the higher levels of 3 and 5 respectively;
❑ sporting successes;
❑ number of exclusions;
❑ incidence of bullying (this will have to be measurable);
❑ number of lunchtime incidents.

All of these rather crude measures do belong in any debate about ethos, effectiveness and what makes a good, successful and positive school. The danger is, however, that crude methods will also be adopted to collect evidence of any other indicators which may be more complex than simple measurable statistics.

What needs to be recognised is that defining, developing and building up a positive and welcoming ethos that does raise standards is not simple at all. It is a difficult and sensitive issue that all headteachers have to grasp, hold and twist into shape.

THE SCHOOL'S AIMS STATEMENT

What the school needs to say about teaching, learning and the curriculum will be examined in the next chapter and there will be an inevitable overlap between them and the school's overall aims statement.

Each school has to have a brochure or prospectus about the school. This is to market the school in a positive way to parents and to anyone else who has a legitimate reason to read it. Many schools extend this and are producing Web sites that make access to details about the school much easier and to a much wider audience. There is little point in detailing what has to be in the brochure because much of it is information that is statutory. Each prospectus or brochure has to have an aims statement which outlines the basic principles that govern the school's ethos. In many ways the general aims statement should summarise how the school works and what it intends to do in such a way that teachers, governors and parents are able to understand the school's intentions and how it will achieve them. Table 1.4 has three examples of aims statements. They don't claim to be definitive statements but should suggest ways of summarising the aims in a simple and easy to understand way.

I won't analyse the aims statements in any great detail. You must reach your own decisions about what is important to say about your school. These decisions must be agreed with all stakeholders, such as teachers, parents and governors, and must be reviewed regularly. It is no good if the head writes it and then expects everyone else to agree with it. It has to be an agreed whole school statement because the aims statement defines the 'quality' of what is being offered. This being the case, it is important to identify some of the core issues that the three examples identify. They are:

❏   confident individuals, ie children who are able to make choices;
❏   children who are encouraged to fulfil their potential and achieve personal success;
❏   highly motivated independent learners;
❏   a balanced curriculum including the National Curriculum.

The aims statement and 'quality'

Most aims statements will include some or all of the above and need to be written so that parents as 'customers' can understand, agree with and empathise with the main issues in such a way that they send their children to your school. The 'quality' of the school is largely defined by the customers. A vocal and supportive group of parents will enthuse the school with an energy that will make it move forward in a positive way in a process of continuous improvement. The quality of the school will then be seen as everybody's responsibility with a team of people, teachers, children, governors and parents being the most powerful agents for accepting the broad aims and delivering the quality that is inherent within them. The ethos within the school, which is defined by its aims, is paramount to raising standards.

Table 1.4 *Aims statements*

Example 1	Everyone who works in the school will aim to create an ethos which will encourage confident, articulate and happy children and where each child will be able to fulfil his or her all-round potential.
	As a school, we intend to inspire every pupil to be a highly motivated, independent learner, who actively participates in a balanced, relevant and well matched curriculum which affords equal opportunities to all. We aim for high standards of self-discipline at all times.
Example 2	In our school we aim to:

> ❑ provide opportunities for individual learning, and the physical and emotional needs of all pupils for whom we have a responsibility so that they can both recognise and achieve personal success;
> ❑ provide a broad and balanced curriculum which is relevant within a stimulating positive and supportive environment;
> ❑ create a school ethos that is firmly based on mutual trust, respect and tolerance;
> ❑ encourage caring and thoughtful attitudes;
> ❑ nurture confidence and independence;
> ❑ empower pupils to make decisions and choices.

Example 3	The school will commit itself to create a harmonious and stimulating environment in which all children will be encouraged to achieve their maximum potential in terms of skills, knowledge and understanding. Each child will be offered opportunities to take decisions, use his or her judgement, work cooperatively with others and develop as a confident individual. We aim to provide a broad and balanced curriculum which incorporates the requirements of the national curriculum.

The aims statement as a model for improvement

In Example 3 in Table 1.4, one of the stated aims is: 'Each child will be offered opportunities to take decisions, use his or her judgement, work cooperatively with others and develop as a confident individual'. During the discussions that take place when the aims statement is being written and certainly when it is in place, it is essential that questions are asked about how this is going to be achieved and what needs to happen in order to meet the demands of the aims statement. What is stated in the whole school aims statement, which will also be implicit in the ethos of the school, has to be seen to mean something. It cannot just exist as a meaningless list of high ideals. What the school is saying that it is trying to do – and the aims statement encapsulates this – should be reflected in what it is actually doing. In successful and effective schools this will be reflected in the School Development Plan, the curriculum and teaching and learning statements, staff development, teaching styles and how staff development and training link to the needs of the school. In other words, while the aims statement may present a broad view of what the school is about, it is the starting point for change, improvement and a way of working. Figure 1.1 is a model of school improvement that uses the aims statement as a starting and finishing point. This particular model reflects many of the issues that this book will be raising and discussing.

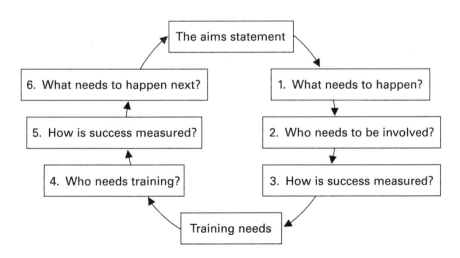

Figure 1.1 *A model for school improvement*

Let's look briefly at each section and the way the aims statement is at the centre of any plan to improve schools and raise attainment:

1. **What needs to happen?** – The aims statement will have identified what the school intends doing and here it is important to develop the 'Plan', which is the School Development Plan and which will break down the broad swathe of ideas and ideals in the aims statement into manageable chunks and an equally manageable time frame.
2. **Who needs to be involved?** – Within the School Development Plan an identified person, who will almost certainly be either a teacher, deputy or the headteacher, must take responsibility for their area of the plan. The idea behind identifying a specific person is that no single person can possibly be expected to control everything that is in the plan and that subject coordinators have to be responsible for the quality of their own subjects. Similarly, no section of the plan that will meet the needs of the aims statement can possibly be left without anyone having ultimate responsibility.
3. **How is success measured?** – This is basically about the monitoring and evaluation of what is being completed in the plan. The basic questions that need to be asked and then answered are: 'How will we know when this area has been completed? How will we know when it has been successful?'
    Training needs – This area of school improvement has already been briefly mentioned and will be considered in Chapter 2. The training and staff development needs will have been identified during performance management reviews and they will be directly linked to the School Development Plan, which is itself linked to the broad aims statement.
4. **Who needs training?** – This is relatively easy to find out because names alongside School Development Plan issues and performance management reviews will have created a list of names matched against training needs.
5. **How is success measured?** – Some kind of pro forma needs to exist which will allow the quality of the training to be measured. On this form should be a section that asks the teacher who has been trained the question: 'What will you be able to do as a result of this training?' The training is effective if the teacher can produce an action plan that will help meet the deadline and achieve success with the area of the School Development Plan for which they are responsible.
6. **What needs to happen next?** – The simplest answer is that the process has to continue. It is a continuous cycle. The broad swathe of issues in the aims statement which determine the school's ethos should remain relatively unchanged within the School Development Plan. However,

in the fine detail, there will always be room for improvement and the need to change. 'What happens next?' is really about the ability to identify the fine detail in a structured way so that the next important steps are taken to raise standards.

THE SCHOOL DEVELOPMENT PLAN

This is the key document that the school needs to drive it forward. It involves areas where standards have to be both maintained and improved. In non-educational management terms this division can be broken down into the concept of the development plan having issues that are 80 per cent maintenance and 20 per cent improvement. Earlier sections of this chapter have identified the School Development Plan (SDP) as supporting the ethos of the school and determining the effectiveness of its drive to raise standards. Added to every school's development plan is its post-Ofsted Action Plan, which should exist as a separate document immediately after an inspection and possibly during the first year of its implementation, but eventually it should be merged with the SDP into one coherent improvement document.

The planning cycle

In the 'model for school improvement' in Figure 1.1, the SDP was identified as playing a leading role in numbers 1, 2 and 3 of the model. It is important to recognise that the process of development planning is cyclical. Each aspect of the cycle – planning, implementing, monitoring and evaluating – requires quality time. Figure 1.2 suggests what the planning cycle should include.

The planning cycle involves the following:

- Looking back at any previous plans.
- Checking that what is being said about the school in the aims statement still holds true.
- Developing the plan.
- Matching the plan with any budgetary implications, making sure that whatever training is necessary for the success of the plan is built into it.
- Implementing the plan (the planning cycle is an annual event, so whatever is planned needs to have a clear completion date).
- Monitoring and evaluating the plan. This will feed into the next planning cycle.

Figure 1.2 *The school development planning cycle*

The planning process

It is important that the SDP should not be devised solely by the headteacher
or the headteacher and deputy. By involving all teachers, parents and
governors, the school will be able to take advantage of wider expertise
and knowledge. The drawback is that the more people involved, the
slower the process; however, the end product will be owned by everyone
and is more likely to be accepted and made to work. In *Development
Planning: A Practical Guide* (DES, 1991), it is suggested that the SDP 'is a
plan of needs for development set in the context of the school's aims and
values, its existing achievements and national and LEA policies and
initiatives. Detailed objectives are set for one year and the objectives for
later years are sketched in outline'. In fact, most SDPs are for three years
with a review each year. This means that while the planning is cyclical,
each year the plan is also pushed forward so that within three years, if
there aren't too many new initiatives, all of the original plan will have been
completed.

Careful planning

It seems unreasonable to expect a positive ethos to arise out of random events. There has to be committed and detailed planning. The changes confronting schools are too great to expect the challenges they present to be successfully met without careful planning. Similarly, the drive to raise standards and achieve total quality is such a key issue that there must be committed and detailed whole school planning. Smith (1995) in *Successful School Management* suggests: 'If random elements are allowed to be the main method of planning and decision making, then they will inevitably become the "norm" and everyone will be so overloaded and confused by an unplanned mass of competing priorities that nothing of value will emerge and nothing that has been written in the plan will be sustained' (1995: 41).

The purpose of development planning

What is most important is that school development planning clarifies thinking and identifies development and management tasks which are compatible with the stated aims and ethos of the school. It provides a sense of direction and a clear focus for work within the school. Most schools view the school development plan as a working document that allows them to escape from crisis management and to plan for the future in a way that will diminish the number or impact of crises. It is also an organisational tool enabling everyone who is involved in it to be efficient and clear about what they are doing and why. In many ways it is a means to developing both a short, in terms of one year, and long, in terms of three years, vision.

Writing the plan

Writing the plan can be easier if it is based on the following structure, which is partly identified as a practical way forward in *Development Planning: A Practical Guide* (DES, 1991). Many of the suggestions can be related to Figure 1.2:

1. Evidence is collected which identifies the school's needs. This is usually done by taking an audit of the school's strengths and weaknesses as well as including any items left over from a previous plan or any important tasks that are in the school's post-Ofsted action plans.
2. Priorities are established from the audit, ie a list is made of what has been identified as needing to be done in order to continue the school's

positive ethos or to improve it by more structured and organised planning. These priorities will fit into the plan's three-year cycle.
3. Priorities must be made manageable in terms of time, ie how the first year is written in detail and the subsequent years in outline.
4. The following points have to be included within the plan:
    ❏ what the task is;
    ❏ what exactly needs to be done, ie the actions;
    ❏ who needs to be involved, ie the owner of the task;
    ❏ completion date of the task;
    ❏ how progress and completion will be monitored;
    ❏ the outcomes, ie how the school will know that the task has been completed and is effective.

In addition to these guidelines for writing the plan, both the cost of each task, if it has a cost, and whether there are training and staff development implications for the task, have to be identified and either written into the plan or planned in detail in another way.

Table 1.5 is an example of development plan headings and suggests an example of what needs to be written. In this example there are just symbols in the text to identify finance and training, eg £££ suggests that for this action there are budgetary implications and # suggests training implications.

Contents of the plan

Table 1.5 identifies just one aspect of a School Development Plan. It is not easy to suggest examples of priorities that will be relevant to large numbers of individual schools but there are certain common areas such as those related to raising standards in core National Curriculum subjects. Some schools will restrict their plan quite narrowly to curriculum and staffing issues, while others will be much more inclusive and will include such areas as the school environment, improving communication between home and school etc. The focus that any school brings to bear on their own plan needs to be on those areas that impact most upon the quality of education, pupils' performance and standards of attainment. The most common areas will include:

❏ curriculum and assessment;
❏ special educational needs;
❏ other whole school issues such as equal opportunities;
❏ staff development;
❏ personnel issues;
❏ parents and the school community;

Table 1.5 *An example of a section from a School Development Plan*

TASK	ACTION	OWNER	COMPLETION	MONITORING	OUTCOMES
Maintain and improve the use of ICT in the curriculum and raise the profile of ICT in teaching and learning.	Create a living school Web site that includes teachers, children, parents and governors. £££###	Janet A	Started February 2001, initial completion January 2002	Termly discussions in staff meeting. Time given in Summer training day and Autumn training day.	We will know that the Web site is successful when it helps market the school and is a place for celebrating the school's achievements and successes.
	Audit staff needs and organise NOF training for all teachers. £££###	Janet A	NOF training begins Autumn 2001	Termly at staff meetings + time given to NOF training meetings.	All teachers will have completed their NOF training and be able to use it in their work in the classroom.
	Complete the ICT scheme of work.	Janet A	By January 2002	Autumn term training day and autumn term governor's curriculum committee.	All teachers will understand the scheme of work and will be using it in their classrooms.

❑ governors;
❑ finance and resources;
❑ buildings, premises, school grounds;
❑ other management issues.

The plan as a working document

If the School Development Plan is the key document in school improvement and raised standards then it has to be seen as a working document that is kept alive and used, changed and modified when and where necessary. There needs to be an attitude to the plan that recognises that it represents 'the life of the school'. The difficulties in making a working document are partly to do with the need to make it clear and understandable and at the same time have a thorough grasp of all the school's needs. It can be a long document and if it has to be, then so be it, but no matter whether it is short or long, it still has to focus attention on the aims of education in the school; to bring together all aspects of a school's planning; to turn long-term visions into short-term action plans; and to give teachers greater control over the nature and pace of change.

The benefits of planning

The main benefit, of course, is that there is a recognisable improvement in the quality of education that the school offers to children, not only in what they learn, but also in what they can achieve. It should not only be the children who benefit from this structured and careful planning. The whole process will help teachers by increasing their confidence, improving the quality of staff development, strengthening the partnership between teaching staff and the governing body, and making it easier to report on the work of the school to anyone who is interested and who needs to know what the school is doing currently and what it intends to achieve in the future. An interesting way to end this section and this chapter would be a reminder that Ofsted can comment on School Development Plans. The following three extracts from Inspection reports are quoted from *The Plan is the School* (WCC, 1998). I have identified some of the key points by using italics:

1. 'The school's development plan is a clear and comprehensive document which sets out long and short term priorities and assesses the cost of these. *All staff are involved in the production of the plan.*'
2. 'The school development plan is clear, carefully costed and *identifies appropriate short and medium term objectives which are then implemented.*'

3.   'The school development plan is a carefully considered document,
     formulated by the head and staff in consultation with the governors. It
     contains realistic targets and provides a clear basis for monitoring the
     progress of various developments. *It has a positive influence on the quality
     of provision and is effective in directing available resources.* Targets identified
     in the school development plan are being realised systematically.'

IMPORTANT POINTS

The ethos, aims statement and development plan are bound together in
ways that influence many aspects of school management, teaching and
learning. Some of the important points raised in this chapter and which
will form part of later chapters include:

❏   The ethos has to be positive and it has to be owned by all the staff. It is
    no good if the headteacher is trying to impose his or her own ethos on
    a reluctant staff.
❏   The ethos has to be sold to the community and most of all to parents.
    Its broad swathe of information about how the school functions needs
    to be attractive to parents whose support is essential if the school is to
    thrive and remain successful.
❏   Leadership is essential in making sure that the right ethos is achieved.
    This should be collegial rather than autocratic.
❏   There are many contributory factors to a positive ethos including what
    happens in classrooms, eg good teaching will be a positive influence
    on everything that happens in school as will forward planning, profes-
    sional development and the organisation of routine administration.
❏   The aims statement is a general view of how the school will function.
    It is a vision of the future and defines the quality of the school.
❏   The aims statement also has to be the focal point of the School Develop-
    ment Plan. Any plans to improve the school have to be related to what
    the school's aims are.
❏   In the cycle of development planning it is important to identify the
    actions that have to be taken; who has to take them; the time span for
    completion; how the actions will be monitored and evaluated and how
    the school will know that what has been planned is successful.
❏   An effective plan will have been developed and written by the head-
    teacher, all teachers and governors.
❏   Most of all it will, like the ethos and the aims statement, be a working
    tool for raising standards.

2

STAFF DEVELOPMENT AND THE TEACHING AND LEARNING POLICY

The key features of an effective school are to raise standards and encourage learning throughout life. This will mean that everyone needs to develop their learning and thinking skills if they are to be effective learners in the future. It is important that children experience success in learning as well as being able to recognise the relevance of learning. In an improving school there will be an ethos where staff are valued and where the development and training needs are met. This has nothing to do with headteachers being altruistic but all to do with the need to recruit and retain the best staff possible. In Chapter 1 it was suggested that the most valuable resources in any school are the adults who work there, and it is important to make sure that their skills are developed. All staff should be entitled to training, not only to do their present job but also as preparation for their future development. If this is the case, then it also follows that the ethos of the school must suggest that there is a belief in people and in their ability to learn, develop and grow.

IDENTIFYING TRAINING AND STAFF DEVELOPMENT NEEDS

The two main ways of identifying training needs are: 1) performance management, where targets are set and the kind of training necessary to meet the targets is identified; 2) the School Development Plan, where it is useful to identify the training implications of specific tasks that have to be completed.

Both performance management and development planning are formal processes which involve all staff, and their relationship with training and development will be discussed in detail later in the chapter. There are also other sources of information that the headteacher can use to identify and analyse training needs. They include:

❏ **Staffing** – Training may well be influenced by the teaching staff that are available. For example, newly qualified teachers will need specific training related to their inexperience. If a teacher is moving from one year group to another, or one key stage to another, they will need training that is specifically related to the ages of the children that they are teaching.

❏ **Attainment** – If the national test results are poor in a particular area, eg writing in Key Stage 1, then it is logical to develop a training programme that will help address some of the problems.

❏ **Parental feedback** – It is important to satisfy the needs of both children and parents, if this is at all possible. If, during a parental questionnaire, for example, it is obvious that there are concerns about lunchtime supervision, then it is logical that some kind of training for lunchtime supervisors might be appropriate.

❏ **Current training provision** – Current training and staff development need to be monitored and evaluated regularly. This may identify gaps in the provision of training in both the kinds of courses on offer and who has gone to them. If there is criticism about some of the training that is offered, then who provides the training might need to be changed.

❏ **Staff retirement** – This is related to 'staffing' and staff development because it is important to plan for retirements so that lost skills are replaced or, if the skills are not directly replaced by recruitment, they can be replaced by training other colleagues.

❏ **Current problems** – There may be a current problem that has only just been identified. For example, boys' attainment in writing in Key Stage 2 may have suddenly been identified as very low when compared to that of girls. This will mean that there is a need for some training on raising boys' achievement in this area.

❏ **Change** – This has had to be faced by schools over and over again in the past few years. Much of this change has meant that there has been a need for more staff development. For example, the literacy and numeracy strategies have generated an enormous amount of training, sometimes at the expense of other subjects.

❏ **Skill levels** – As the nature of teaching changes, so do the skills that are required. This is especially true in ICT. In many schools, this has meant that there has had to be an audit of staff skills, so that specific training can be arranged.

❏ **Money** – Training and staff development cost money. This is certainly the case for those courses that take place during the school day in teachers' quality time. It is important that schools make sure that all their available standards fund money is used to maintain the progress of staff development and training.

(More details of these issues can be found in Smith R, *Making your School More Successful Pack 2* (Pearson Publishing, 2001).)

Performance management

This is one of the main formal processes for identifying staff training needs. What is also very important is that it is a shared process. It is not imposed by headteachers and team leaders but is partly driven by the needs of teachers. It will improve good practice for everyone because it makes every teacher and headteacher set targets and discuss how they will meet them. Part of this discussion will identify the kind of training and development that is necessary.

The performance management process is cyclical and Figure 2.1 shows this. It basically consists of the following elements:

1. Headteachers or designated team leaders (usually deputies and senior teachers) will meet each teacher and set targets for the year, identifying training needs that will help meet the targets.
2. Both the teacher and team leader will review progress regularly. This will mean classroom observations, monitoring targets and checking that training is available.
3. In the following year, ie a year after the review meeting, there will be a meeting to review achievements and to discuss how successful and effective the training was. This meeting will then set targets for the next performance management cycle.

Another example of a performance management cycle can be found in *Teachers: Meeting the Challenge of Change* (DfEE/HMSO, 1998).

Targets and training needs

As you can see from Figure 2.1, targets and training needs are discussed and identified during the initial meeting of the cycle. It is important to continue examining them together, because they are closely linked and the targets set will largely determine the training needs of individual teachers.

Table 2.1 is an example of a list of targets agreed during a performance management review for a Year 6 teacher.

It should be relatively easy to match the targets to what this teacher needs in terms of training and staff development. Table 2.2 identifies specific training for the same Year 6 teacher as Table 2.1 and, at the same time, suggests what should be achieved by the training. I think it is important to

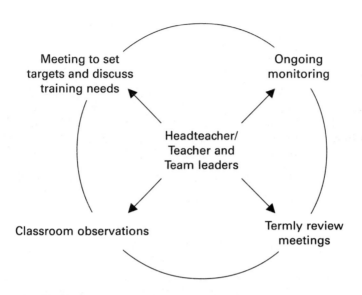

Figure 2.1 *The performance management cycle*

Table 2.1 *Performance management targets*

Name of teacher _____ Date of meeting _____

TARGETS	WHAT WILL BE ACHIEVED
1. Raise the attainment in English in my class by 4% in reading for girls and 3% in reading for boys. 2. Raise the attainment in writing for both boys and girls by 4%.	An improvement in Year 6 national test scores and more parents being satisfied with the results.
3. Improve my basic ICT skills on how to use the networked computers that are available.	ICT will be used more effectively in my classroom in more national curriculum subjects.
4. Improve my team leader skills of discussing progress and needs, target setting, and lesson observation and feedback.	I will perform more successfully during the performance management process.
5. Improve my organisational skills and time management.	Better organised classroom and more effective at clearing my desk and completing all priority tasks.

identify all training needs during the review meeting. This, of course, does not mean that all the training will take place. Individual needs will have to be balanced against each other, against the needs of the school development plan and against the constraints of the budget that is available for training. At the beginning of the next performance management cycle, what has been achieved against the targets will be discussed and, inevitably, if any haven't been met it is important to ask whether there is a link between this and a failure to find suitable training. If this is the case, there are important questions to be asked about the budget for training and/or the training that is actually available.

Table 2.2 *Training and staff development opportunities*

TRAINING MATCHED TO TARGETS	WHAT WILL BE ACHIEVED
Specific training in techniques for teaching reading and writing for Year 6 children.	This should help with strategies for improving test scores.
Courses on classroom techniques for raising boys' achievement.	If I know what might work in the classroom it might raise boys' test scores.
Basic skills course in using Windows, Word and Sims Assessment Manager.	Understanding how to use the computer more effectively will mean that I can work alongside children with more confidence.
Courses on how to be an effective performance manager team leader, including classroom observation and feedback after observations.	I need help to make sure that effective targets are set for teachers for whom I am a team leader. I also need to be sure that I am able to identify strengths and weaknesses in teaching and that I am able to feed these back to the teachers concerned.
Courses and training on time management.	I need to improve how I prioritise my work and learn how to complete important tasks and leave less important ones until later and yet still complete them within a specific period of time.

The School Development Plan

Development planning was dealt with in some detail in Chapter 1 but it would be disappointing to think that the targets set by individual teachers in the performance management cycle were much different from the actions identified in the development plan. The sample planning sheet in Table 1.5 identified several actions that were assigned to a specific teacher. They included creating a Web site and an ICT scheme of work together with completion dates. If those dates were within a performance management cycle then they should be set as targets together with appropriate training. What will not appear on the development plan that is applicable to every individual teacher and has to be included in the performance management review is a target linked to raising achievement within each teacher's class.

The headteacher's performance management

Headteachers themselves will also be part of performance management and it is equally true that the targets that they have to meet will also need the support of training. Heads will have their performance measured against the targets set by the governing body. This will work in a similar cycle to the performance management of teachers in that performance against the targets will be measured each year. These targets will include:

❏ school leadership and management;
❏ pupil progress;
❏ personal professional development.

Governors can be helped with this process by external advisers but in agreeing the objectives, key points for governors to bear in mind are:

❏ The headteacher's personal contribution to meeting targets which affect the school's performance.
❏ There should be between three and five agreed targets or objectives.
❏ Targets should not be too narrowly defined.
❏ Targets (and this is similar to those for teachers) should relate to the actions identified in the School Development Plan and any post-Ofsted Action Plans.
❏ Targets should be relevant to both the needs of the school and those of the headteacher.
❏ There should be measurable outcomes for each objective so that all parties are clear about what evidence will be used to evaluate performance.

❑ Targets should relate to available training and should not be such that to meet them there would have to be an unreasonable amount of training needed.

One key aspect of staff development and training that applies directly to headteachers and has a direct bearing on issues raised in this chapter is the headteacher's actual ability to meet the requirements of his or her statutory responsibilities in the areas of performance management and staff development.

Statutory responsibilities and existing practice for headteachers

As part of a process of school improvement there are already statutory responsibilities for headteachers which include: 1) evaluating the standards of teaching and learning in the school; 2) ensuring that proper standards of professional performance are established.

In other words, performance management, the quality and standards of teaching and learning, and the training and development needs that are necessary to 'ensure that proper standards of professional performance are established' are closely intertwined. Many of these strategies will already be happening in effective schools. They fall into the category of existing good practice and are summarised in Smith R, *Performance Management and Threshold Assessment Pack 1* (Pearson, 2000). They include:

❑ an agreed system of classroom observation and feedback;
❑ work trawls to assess attainment and progression;
❑ effective school development plans with staff development opportunities identified;
❑ target setting as an approach to raising standards and improving pupil progress.

There will also be a system of good professional practice which will be a key part of the performance management process. This will include:

❑ an annual review of teachers' job descriptions;
❑ prioritising tasks for the year;
❑ allocating resources;
❑ identifying professional development needs;
❑ professional reviews and action plans.

It is important for headteachers to look at the current practice in their schools and to audit the relationship between performance management, development planning and staff development. If an external and more structured audit is needed, there are other methods in *Inspecting Schools: Handbook for Inspecting Primary and Nursery Schools* (HMSO, 1999), together with the CD ROM supplied with the *Handbook*. If we need to identify some final characteristics of existing best practice in terms of effective school improvement, it should include:

❑   a commitment by all staff to raising attainment;
❑   a culture where teachers are valued for the essential part they play in pupils' welfare and in raising standards;
❑   an ethos of trust between the headteacher, senior managers and teachers which allows critical judgements about quality to be made;
❑   an awareness that *staff development* has a crucial role to play in raising standards.

A staff development policy

All schools will develop staff and all teachers will receive training of some kind. This will have been happening in all kinds of ways for many years. By linking training to the school's development plan and to performance management, staff development becomes part of the school's formal processes of improvement and raising standards. As soon as this becomes the case, it is important to make a formal statement of intent in the form of a policy which will set out exactly what the school intends to do.

There are many ways of developing such a policy to reflect what an individual school needs. As with other policies, everyone needs to be involved and governors should be aware, not only of the training that takes place but of the policy that formalises the process.

Table 2.3 summarises the framework for such a policy under various important and useful headings. It is important to notice that the policy applies to all staff. Many schools will have started extending their performance management policy to teaching assistants and administrative staff and development planning may well also apply to those same non-teaching staff. They are all crucial members of the whole school team and, if they are to remain effective, they also need to be trained to do their jobs successfully.

Table 2.3 *Staff development policy*

1. Introduction	All staff working in the school are entitled to a framework of support to enable them to develop effectively within their role in the school. This support will be offered both from within the school, by sharing expertise with colleagues, reading appropriate journals and teaching materials, working alongside colleagues, attending external courses and using staff meetings and training days as forums for staff development, and by using visiting trainers.
2. Purposes of staff development and training	Staff development is seen as a way of making all staff feel confident to be effective in meeting the needs of their role, to enable staff to solve problems of practice or school management and to empower staff to maintain what is effective and to manage improvements and change.
3. Identifying training and development needs	Training and development needs will be identified in the following ways: ❏ the school development plan and any post-Ofsted Action Plan; ❏ performance management and any individual action plans related to the development plan; ❏ the headteacher's and senior teacher's perceptions of identified needs after discussions with subject coordinators; ❏ any imposed changes that require training. (Past examples have included literacy, numeracy and performance management.)
4. Staff development and training routes	Development and training will be provided through various means, including: ❏ support in school via the expertise of colleagues, subject coordinators, staff meetings, working alongside colleagues, reading appropriate journals and other teaching materials, senior teacher meetings, working parties and performance management reviews;

Table 2.3 *(Contd)*

	❏ invited speakers during training days;
	❏ courses arranged by the LEA;
	❏ inspectors' feedback and advice supporting individual teachers and curriculum coordinators on teaching quality;
	❏ appropriate courses from other authorities and other organisations;
	❏ visits to other schools and meetings in school such as full governors and governors' sub committees.
5. Resources for professional development and training	The resources fall into three broad categories:
	❏ budget funding, ie a percentage of the budget is allocated for staff training;
	❏ time allocation and commitment to training and development at meetings and on training days;
	❏ allocated funds, eg standards grants to be used to pay for courses and teacher cover.
6. Monitoring and evaluation	❏ Staff development and training will be evaluated annually within the performance management cycle.
	❏ Details of staff development and training will be reported to the governors annually.
	❏ Staff attending external courses will be required to feed back information to all staff.
	❏ A course evaluation pro forma will be completed after each course. One copy will be kept centrally and one in the teacher's own professional development portfolio.
7. Success criteria	❏ Standards will be raised because of improved knowledge of the teaching and learning process.
	❏ There will be increased staff awareness of training and development needs.
	❏ Increased staff confidence.
	❏ Training needs identified in the development plan and in performance management are met.

EFFECTIVE TEACHING AND LEARNING

We need to refer back to Chapter 1 and the ethos and aims statement of the school. Each school has different and often unique characteristics which influence the curriculum it provides (this will be discussed in Chapter 8) and the teaching and learning that takes place. The aims statement makes explicit the values that underpin teaching and learning and the school's aims are reflected in the ethos which influences the working relationships of those who are in school every day. The ethos of the school will have a significant impact on raising pupil achievement because the way staff and children feel about themselves affects the way they are able to participate in school life and also influences strategies that are in place for teaching and learning.

What is effective learning?

The National Curriculum Handbook (HMSO, 1999) has this to say about learning:

> Learning is a means of encouraging and stimulating the best possible progress and the highest attainment for all pupils. It should build on pupils' strengths, interests and experiences and develop their confidence in their capacity to learn and work independently and collaboratively. It should equip them with the essential learning skills of literacy, numeracy and information and communication technology, and promote an enquiring mind and capacity to think rationally.

In *Teaching for Effective Learning: A Paper for Discussion and Development* (SCAA, 1999), there are several useful suggestions that relate to trying to define what learning is. They include:

> We are more likely to learn when we are motivated to do so. Young people who feel good about themselves are much more likely to be highly motivated to learn.

> We can learn how to learn by developing skills which help us to think, feel and act more effectively.

It is obvious to all teachers that children learn in different ways. Some learn best through *visual* stimulus, eg diagrams, videos, written words, and others through *auditory* means, eg lectures, discussion and listening to colleagues.

Some children are *kinaesthetic* learners who respond well to hands-on activities, movement and drama.

Teachers need to provide for a range of learning styles to be met and Table 2.4 suggests that the best learning will frequently have certain specified and identifiable characteristics.

Table 2.4 *Learning characteristics*

Effective learning has many, if not all the following characteristics:

❏ The individual learning needs of children are met.
❏ A clear sense of purpose is shared with the learner.
❏ New learning is placed in the context of previous experience.
❏ New learning is applied to other situations.
❏ Children who are confident about what they are expected to do, and are set tasks which extend their learning.
❏ Children who are able to work individually, in groups and in the community to consider the implications of new learning for themselves, for society and for the environment.
❏ Children who are able to take some responsibility for their own learning and behaviour.
❏ Children who are able to appreciate the continuity in their learning.
❏ Children who are able to learn in a variety of ways including visually, auditory and kinaesthetically.

What is effective teaching?

Let's start this brief section (there will be further discussion in Chapter 7) on teaching by summarising Ofsted's expectations. In *Inspecting Schools: Handbook for Inspecting Primary and Nursery Schools* (1999) they suggest the following:

Inspectors must evaluate and report on:

❏ The quality of teaching, judged in terms of its impact on pupils' learning and what makes it successful or not. Inspectors must include evaluations of:
  – how well the skills of literacy and numeracy are taught, particularly to pupils of primary ages. . . whose reading and writing or numeracy are poor;

> – how well the school meets the needs of all its pupils, taking account of age, gender, ethnicity, capability, special educational needs, gifted and talented pupils and those for whom English is an additional language.
> ❑ The teaching in each subject, commenting on any variations between subjects and year groups.
> ❑ How well pupils learn and make progress.

In other words, effective teaching according to Ofsted has to have an impact and how effective that impact is will depend on how well teachers relate to the children in their classrooms. What teachers actually do is very important, and the quality of teaching, which is the subject of Chapter 7, is a crucial factor in promoting effective learning in schools. The success of the teaching that takes place can be affected by several factors:

❑ the learning environment – where this is the case, it is important to make sure that the ethos of the school supports successful learning and effective teaching;
❑ the resources available to support learning;
❑ the planning that goes into the lesson;
❑ what the teacher does during the lesson.

While teachers certainly bring their own personal style to teaching, it is important that they are able to absorb and use different teaching strategies which they personalise and then use as their own style. Table 2.5 summarises some ideas about 'good' teaching. It does this within a framework where the effectiveness of what happens in the classroom is defined by teachers having both the right and responsibility to develop a climate in their classroom that not only supports effective learning but involves maintaining order without undermining children's self-esteem.

Teaching and learning processes

All 'good' schools have to take the view that teaching and learning processes are as significant as curriculum content in determining and influencing pupils' progress and achievement. Having considered learning and teaching separately, it is important to make sure that the two aspects make a coherent whole. In addition to the links between teaching and learning, there are also very significant links between teaching, learning and behaviour. The Elton Report, for example, makes very clear the strong influence that a teacher's general competence has on the behaviour of pupils in the class.

Table 2.5 *Effective teaching*

The best teaching is likely to occur when:

❑ There is a clear identification of learning objectives.
❑ The learning experience is appropriate to the children's stage of development and maturity.
❑ The selected strategy is appropriate to the learning purpose of the lesson.
❑ A teacher's lesson plan takes account of the range of ability in the class and strategies are used which ensure that every child is challenged and at the same time has opportunities to succeed.
❑ Planning includes consideration of how the time available is to be managed and by whom.
❑ The teacher regularly assesses and records the progress children make, as well as their achievements, and uses assessment outcomes to plan the next stage of learning.
❑ The teacher has clear expectations of the children, which are shared with them.
❑ The teacher communicates clearly with the children.
❑ There is an atmosphere of trust and respect throughout the lesson.
❑ All adults in the classroom are able to carry out their roles confidently and competently.

Table 2.6 suggests some of the clear links between teaching and learning that have to be considered before developing a teaching and learning policy. It will be interesting to refer back to Tables 2.4 and 2.5 to see how the two elements are brought together because it is inevitable that there will be some areas that overlap and some that are repeated.

If it is possible to summarise what happens in an effective classroom, then it is possible to link successful learning to good teaching. For example, children will be more successful learners and make good progress if the teaching makes sure that they are:

❑ provided with activities that ensure they are learning the right things suitable for their age;
❑ clear about the objectives of the lesson and what needs to be done;
❑ able to understand how they can improve their work;
❑ understanding what they are doing;
❑ finding tasks demanding but achievable with effort on their part;
❑ getting the appropriate help when it is needed;

Table 2.6 *Teaching and learning characteristics*

The school and teacher will aim to:

❑ promote the view that learning should be enjoyable, engaging, rewarding and confidence building;

❑ regard assessment as an integral and valuable element of the learning process in order to diagnose difficulties and plan for progress;

❑ recognise that children have individual needs and, if they are to influence their own learning, must have appropriate opportunities to make decisions about what is learnt;

❑ offer intellectual challenge for children and set them achievable learning goals;

❑ encourage children to work both individually and in groups in order to foster both independence and cooperation;

❑ encourage and enable children to experience things at first hand and have the opportunity to reflect on their experience;

❑ provide relevant activities to enable skills to be practised and applied in 'authentic' situations;

❑ recognise that parents and families play a part in educating their children and so provide opportunities for their involvement;

❑ develop clear and concise records of educational achievement as a means of recording and acknowledging children's experiences and achievements;

❑ plan homework as an integral part of the curriculum and consistent with the school's policy on homework.

❑ staying on task;
❑ maintaining a good work rate;
❑ well motivated.

Children will be less successful learners and make less progress if they are:

❑ not sure about the lesson's objectives and what they are supposed to be doing;
❑ given purposeless activities;
❑ given activities from which they cannot improve;
❑ finding the work too difficult;
❑ finding the work too easy;
❑ unsure of how to improve and what to do to improve;

❑ expected to work at too fast a pace for their ability;
❑ expected to work at too slow a pace for their ability;
❑ poorly motivated.

THE TEACHING AND LEARNING POLICY

So far in this section of this chapter, there have been many suggestions related to what is effective teaching and learning. They now need to be brought together into a coherent policy which will provide the appropriate guidelines for all teachers and teaching assistants to follow. In order to develop the policy effectively you will need to consider:

❑ an agreed definition of teaching and learning;
❑ how this definition links to the school's aims statement;
❑ the values and ethos that underpins the way the school works;
❑ how the needs of all learners will be met;
❑ the skills of individual staff.

For a policy to be successful it needs to be accessible to all readers. In order to do this schools should:

❑ avoid the use of jargon;
❑ produce a clear and structured policy;
❑ make sure that it is useful for class teachers, subject coordinators and senior teachers;
❑ have links to and implications for such other areas of the school as development planning, performance management and professional development.

It is also the case that an effective policy is one that is meaningful, easily understood and readily implemented. Because it offers each teacher a consistent approach to a particular subject or area of school development, it should mean that all teachers are able to promote the learning of all children. If learning is our most important aim as teachers, then teaching is our most important activity. While the policy should be a structured way to promote a consistent approach, we shouldn't lose sight of the fact, already mentioned in this chapter, that teachers also need the freedom to be able to use their own enthusiasm, ideas, personal style and professional knowledge.

Table 2.7 suggests the framework for a teaching and learning policy. It is similar to Table 2.3 in that if the sections are put together with modifications made to reflect your particular circumstances, it is possible to use it as a basis for a whole school policy.

Table 2.7 *Teaching and learning policy*

1. Introduction	The main aim of this policy is to enable each child to reach his or her maximum potential. To do this a peaceful environment has to be created in which tolerance, mutual cooperation and stability are encouraged so that each child can work productively, learn to make decisions, use his or her own judgement and cooperate courteously with others. As a school we are trying to achieve these high standards by responding professionally, sensitively and caringly to the needs of all our pupils.
	Within these broad guidelines, teaching and learning has to take place as effectively as possible.
2. Broad aims of the teaching and learning policy	Teaching and learning within the school will:
	❏ raise levels of attainment for all children;
	❏ develop confident, disciplined and enquiring learners;
	❏ foster a love of learning;
	❏ raise self-esteem;
	❏ increase personal responsibility;
	❏ ensure equal opportunities in relation to gender, race, class, ability, belief and culture;
	❏ provide a safe and happy work place.
3. Equal opportunities	All children in the school must be given full access to the curriculum, including the national curriculum, and all staff will endeavour to help all children reach their full potential regardless of race, gender, age or ability.
4. What each teacher will aim to do	Each teacher will aim to:
	❏ show good subject knowledge and understanding in the way they present and discuss their subject;

43

Table 2.7 *(Contd)*

❑ show their technical competence in teaching phonics and all basic skills;

❑ plan effectively, setting clear objectives that all children understand;

❑ challenge and inspire children and expect the most of them, so as to deepen their knowledge and understanding;

❑ use a wide range of teaching methods that will enable all children to learn effectively;

❑ manage children well and insist on high standards of behaviour;

❑ use time, support staff and other resources, especially information technology, effectively;

❑ assess children's work thoroughly and use assessments to help and encourage children to overcome difficulties;

❑ use homework effectively to reinforce and/or extend what is learnt in school.

5. What will be expected of each child

Each teacher will expect all children to:

❑ acquire new knowledge or skills;

❑ develop ideas and increase their understanding;

❑ apply intellectual, physical or creative effort in their work;

❑ be productive and work at a good pace;

❑ show interest in their work;

❑ be able to sustain concentration related to their age and ability;

❑ think and learn for themselves;

❑ understand what they are doing, how well they have done and how they can improve.

6. Expectations in lessons

In each lesson in all subjects, each teacher will ensure that all children are:

1. **learning the right things** by acquiring or consolidating one or more of the key competencies that underpin each subject at a level appropriate to their age;

Table 2.7 *(Contd)*

---

2. **challenged in relation to their earlier work**; pupils should be able to understand and cope successfully with lesson content by using existing intellectual, physical or creative effort;

3. **productive** by working at their optimum pace and staying on task;

4. **motivated** because they ask questions, learn from their mistakes, learn from each other and seek help when needed.

7. Effective learning   All teachers will recognise that learning is more effective when children are:
- ❏ clear about what has to be done;
- ❏ engaged and informed by good teaching or in activities in which they are learning the right things for their age;
- ❏ clear about what they are trying to achieve and how their work can be improved;
- ❏ understanding what they are doing and finding the task demanding but achievable with sustained effort;
- ❏ seeking and gaining help when needed;
- ❏ staying on task and maintaining a good work rate when set challenging tasks to do;
- ❏ well motivated.

8. Effective teaching   All teachers will recognise that learning is less effective when children are:
- ❏ unsure about what they are supposed to be doing;
- ❏ occupied by purposeless teaching or activities from which they cannot improve their standard key competencies;
- ❏ finding work unduly hard, or too easy or restricting;
- ❏ not knowing what to do to improve;
- ❏ asked to work at too slow or too fast a pace;
- ❏ poorly motivated.

Table 2.7 *(Contd)*

9. Monitoring and evaluation	❏ The policy will be monitored once every two years and this will be stated in the school development plan.
	❏ Teaching quality will be monitored at least once each year within the guidelines and confidentiality of the performance management policy and will include classroom observation and feedback discussion.
	❏ Subject coordinators will also monitor the quality of teaching in their subject.
	We will know this policy is working when:
	❏ subject coordinators are satisfied that subjects are being taught well and that standards are being raised across the key stages;
	❏ realistic targets for pupil attainment are being met;
	❏ all children reach realistic and appropriate levels at qca and national tests;
	❏ Ofsted judge that the quality of teaching is 85% + satisfactory or better, with at least 50% of lessons graded good or better.

IMPORTANT POINTS

This chapter has emphasised three major issues that relate to successful schools and to raising standards: the importance of developing staff and providing them with the relevant and appropriate training; the need to have a consistent staff development policy; and the importance of making sure that the school's teaching and learning policy reflects the individual needs of the school. Within these three broad issues are other important points such as:

❏ Staff development and training needs are largely recognised and identified through the School Development Plan and performance management.

❑ It is also important for headteachers and senior teachers to have an overview of such areas as imminent changes that may affect training needs, changes of staff and recruitment of new staff, current skill levels, any problems related to under-performance that training may help minimise.

❑ Performance management is cyclical and the targets that are set will need training so that they can be met.

❑ The School Development Plan should identify individual teachers and the tasks and actions that they are responsible for completing. The targets set in performance management should be similar to the SDP actions and the training and staff development needs identified for individual teachers should be the same or very similar.

❑ Learning has to be identified and the needs of the three main styles, visual, auditory and kinaesthetic, need to be catered for.

❑ It is important to identify the kind of teaching that works best to improve learning and the kind that will have little or no effect.

❑ There is a close link between the ethos and aims statement, effective teaching and learning, and overall standards of behaviour in the school.

❑ There needs to be a clear and concise staff development and separate teaching and learning policy.

❑ Both policies should be used consistently by all teachers and have an influence on how the school operates and how standards are raised.

3

RECRUITING AND MANAGING STAFF

Headteachers play the most important role in recruiting and retaining staff who have the right qualifications, experiences and personal qualities both to enable the school to run as efficiently as possible and to raise standards. It has already been said in earlier chapters that the staff who work in the school are the most valuable resource and the quality of the staff who are recruited will have a significant effect on the quality of education that the school can provide.

There are also other parts to the staffing equation. They include the shortage of applicants to teaching jobs and the quality of the few applicants that are available. The recruitment and retention of teachers and the obvious shortages mean that the process for selection and how the school approaches potential candidates has to be extremely professional and, at the same time, has to make sure that the appropriate candidate is eventually offered the job.

Everard and Morris (1985) suggest that:

> In many ways we should treat people as any other resource, selecting the best people for the purpose we wish to accomplish, and maintaining, improving and adapting the resource as we would a building or piece of equipment to ensure that it meets our needs. However, there is one important difference; people are thinking resources, who, whether we like it or not, will decide jointly with their superiors and colleagues on how their time, energy, knowledge and skills will be used. (1985: 66)

In the reality of today's market economy, coupled with the shortage of teachers, this bleak scenario of people as abstract resources should not conceal the fact that effective school management is not about recruiting individuals who will work in isolation, but about groups and teams working together with a common purpose in mind. The appointment process, however, is only the first step in recruiting high-quality teachers and building effective and successful teams.

If an appointment is not successful, it is difficult, time-consuming and in many ways destructive to invoke sanctions against any 'incompetent', unreasonable or divisive teacher. Schools are very dependent on good selection processes and an effective and continuing programme of staff development. These recruitment structures and strategies are certainly important when staff vacancies arise or when there are opportunities for recruiting new teachers.

THE SELECTION PROCESS

The selection of staff, then, is a systematic process with two key goals: 1) to attract candidates suitable to do the job; 2) to achieve a match between the person and the job which reduces as far as possible the risk of mismatch between the school and the candidate. This identifies the fact that selection is a two-way process and is not just about the headteacher and governors wanting a particular candidate; it is also about the candidate wanting the job and accepting the offer of a job. If this is the case, then it is also true to say that in selecting the right candidate for a particular job, it is important to think about four basic questions:

❑ Do you know what you want?
❑ How do you get the right person to attend for interview?
❑ How do you recognise the right person when you see them?
❑ How do you know that you have got the appointment right?

Knowing what you want

It is very important to ask the question: 'Do we know what we want?' before any action that involves recruitment is made. It might help to invent a scenario to examine this issue in more detail.

Imagine that a member of staff has just got a job at another school. This means that you have a vacancy for the following September. One of the first things to do is to make notes of the skills that you are losing because of the vacancy and the second is to look closely at the school development plan to find out whether there are any specific skills needed in order to complete the plan. What you are doing, in fact, is deciding the nature of the vacancy and in doing this it is important to:

❏ assess the present situation;
❏ look at any needs, eg School Development Plan or at the opportunities that the post may offer;
❏ ask the person who is leaving to write down all the jobs they do and talk to them about their perceptions of the job they are leaving;
❏ talk with other teachers to get an idea of their needs;
❏ talk with the governors.

In previous chapters, it has been suggested that development planning, which produces the School Development Plan, is a fundamental process. When you look at the SDP for the purposes of recruitment it will be useful to ask questions such as:

❏ Where is the school hoping to go?
❏ Where has the school come from?
❏ Where is the school at the present moment?
❏ What is the school currently involved in?
❏ What does the school need to do next?

The selection panel

Once the nature of the post to be filled has been decided, there needs to be a selection panel who will be able to oversee the whole of the selection process from start to finish. This will need to include the headteacher (and where possible the deputy headteacher) and governors. It is usually the case that the more senior the position, the more governors there are who are involved. The first job that the selection panel has to do after they have recognised the job that is available is to be much more specific and define, as exactly as possible, what the job actually is.

Defining the post

The first requirement is a job description that will form the basis of the selection process. This needs to happen even though the actual final working job description will be agreed between the headteacher and the successful candidate. Selection is impossible without specifying details about the job on offer. This means that the preparation of a working job description is central to the whole process because the job advertisement, the selection of appropriate candidates and interview questions will all follow on from a job description that includes:

❏   the job that has to be done;
❏   the context of the school;
❏   the kind of person who is wanted to do it.

Specifying the job and especially the person may sound sterile and impersonal but unless everyone knows the professional qualities that are being sought, there will be problems. The candidates themselves, for example, will find it difficult to work out how they are being judged and the selection panel, unless they agree what they are looking for, may well be looking for very different people.

Figure 3.1 is a brief example of a job description or job specification for use in the selection process. You may well have a different kind of specification that you use successfully. This one is not a definitive version, but it does include some useful suggestions.

Making a short list

Once you know what you want, and the kind of job specification suggested in Figure 3.1 helps you take this decision, you need to make sure that the right candidates are short listed for interview. The next sequence of events will take place in a more public arena as the selection process begins to move out of the school. As this happens you will need to think about:

❏   the job advertisement;
❏   the particulars that will be sent to candidates (including the job specification);
❏   any specific questions that the school wants applicants to write about;
❏   how candidates will be encouraged to make preliminary visits;
❏   references;
❏   short listing;
❏   dates of interviews and the kinds of questions that will be asked.

The job advertisement, application form and references

Advertising teaching posts is expensive, and to attract a wide field of applicants it is necessary to advertise as widely as possible in as many newspapers and journals as the school can afford. All advertisements should be clear and simple. In many LEAs, there will be standard formats that are part of a local agreement with teaching unions. While you may not agree with some of the issues involved, it is important to be seen to be 'fair' in the sense that the job you are advertising meets the requirements of

The appointment is a management post (1 point) for developing numeracy in maths in this large urban primary school, which has 30 per cent of its children on the SEN register. The teaching commitment in the first instance is with a Year 2 class.

We are looking for a person who:

❏ has a clear philosophy and interest in the teaching of numeracy and maths throughout the primary years;

❏ will have been teaching for at least three years and will see this appointment as a stepping stone for further advancement;

❏ is an effective class teacher with high standards of classroom management and control;

❏ is able to design and revise school policies and schemes of work in consultation with senior teachers and the headteacher and deputy headteacher;

❏ understands the numeracy strategy, has had appropriate training and can train others in making this area of the curriculum effective;

❏ understands assessment within the classroom and can contribute to maintaining the school's successes in some areas of the national tests and raising standards in others;

❏ is able to help and advise colleagues;

❏ is willing and able to talk to parents and governors.

Other desirable qualities will include:

❏ the ability to involve others in raising the standards in numeracy and maths;

❏ the ability to consult and take decisions;

❏ the ability to secure the maximum cooperation of others;

❏ awareness of local and national developments beyond the school;

❏ the ability to write effective polices and reports.

Figure 3.1 *Job description*

employment legislation and does not discriminate unfairly against any group of teachers who may wish to apply.

Application forms are usually standard throughout an LEA and are designed to bring out all the factual data needed and also elicit data which may give the selection panel a clue to past behaviours, posts held etc. Bell (1989) recognises that, 'The application form is more valuable than is generally realised. If carefully designed and interpreted, it can provide a wealth of information about a candidate, for example: previous jobs, courses attended, educational background, personal interests etc. Conversely it will prove to be a blunt instrument if these conditions are not fulfilled' (1989: 97).

The selection panel needs to be able to read the application form so that significant issues are raised immediately during the short-listing process. For example, an unexplained break between teaching jobs needs to be investigated and many short-term jobs in a variety of schools may be significant. But, at the same time, there are unpredictable career paths and the selection panel must balance their expectations so that they do not exclude the candidate who has taken time out to do some interesting activity that could make a valuable contribution to the job and to the school.

Many schools are asking for additional information over and above what is written on the application form. All applications have space for candidates to write a 'letter of application' and this should relate to both the information on the form and the information about the school and the job that has been sent to the candidate. Over and above this, candidates can be asked to write no more than 500 words on specific subjects that are related to the job. If you do this, it will provide you with more evidence to help in the selection process and more scope for questions during the actual interview. It is important to ensure that the issues you ask them to write about are relevant to your particular school and to the vacancy.

References are always needed but they can be misleading so it is always useful to provide the person supplying the reference with such information as:

❑ job details and person specification;
❑ the particular issues that you are most interested in;
❑ whether the reference is open to the candidate or closed and only available to the selection panel;
❑ the deadline for the reference with interview dates etc.

When reading references, it is always useful to adopt a more cynical role and ask such questions as: What is missing? Do I really have a positive statement about those criteria that are important?

Selecting the right candidates for interview

Short listing from what is hopefully a large number of potentially suitable candidates is very important and should involve all the people who will be at the interview. The criteria for selection will be to match each candidate against the needs of the school as defined in the job and person specification.

Other criteria that you will want to use that are not related to the specific job will be obvious ones such as rejecting an application form that is grammatically incorrect with several spelling mistakes, written in a handwriting style similar to hieroglyphics. Once there is agreement of a short list of usually no more than six candidates, you need to find some way of identifying the best person for the job that you have available.

This usually happens by:

❏ inviting the short-listed candidates to visit the school;
❏ asking them to give a short presentation to the selection panel on a relevant subject;
❏ formal interview of the candidates by the panel of selectors.

I am going to concentrate on looking more closely at the formal interview, although it is worth looking briefly at the other two methods which can be used alongside the interview.

You will have to take a decision about the policy of making arrangements for candidates to visit the school. Unless all the candidates have the same opportunity and can take advantage of it, it can discriminate against those who live a long way away. An alternative is to offer each short-listed candidate the opportunity to visit the school and use it as their opportunity to find out whether they still want the job rather than as part of the school's selection process.

If you ask candidates to give a short presentation on a given subject, it is important that each candidate has to talk about the same thing. It is equally important that they are given a precise time limit of no more than 10 minutes and very limited use of technical equipment. Schools usually limit this to an OHP or PowerPoint. During the post-interview discussion, it is important to make sure that each candidate's presentation is part of the decision-making process. If it isn't, then there is no point in spending more than an hour listening to all the presentations. In order to focus this discussion, each person on the selection panel should be given a 'crib' sheet which lists some of the key points that the candidates should have made in their presentation. This will mean that there is at least a simple measure which will help in any subsequent discussion.

Interviewers, the interview and the questions

The interview is quite simply the final stage in a process that is designed to find the most appropriate candidate for the post based on all the available evidence. The main reason for holding interviews is to find out which of the candidates best fits the school's needs. It is worth bearing in mind, however, that formal interviews are relatively rare for even the most job-hungry interviewees, and that the formality demands a rather unnatural way of behaving; unless great care is taken, it is possible for the interview to be unreliable.

As far as the interviewers are concerned, this unreliability usually takes the form of:

❑ making hasty and subjective judgements;
❑ failing to ask appropriate questions;
❑ taking small pieces of evidence and expanding them to create negative impressions of a candidate;
❑ spending too long thinking about the next question and failing to listen to the answer to the present one;
❑ not studying the documentation on each candidate in depth.

These kinds of faults can be eliminated, or if not eliminated, greatly reduced, by managing the interview effectively.

The interview should not be an interrogation. Those asking the questions need to think carefully about the type of questions they wish to ask so that they can make sure that they are open ended and require candidates to give explanatory answers. Playfoot, Skelton and Southworth in *The Primary School Management Book* (1989) suggest that good interviewing relies on:

❑ planning the entrance and settling in of the candidate;
❑ controlling the interview so that the candidate is telling you the things you need to know;
❑ letting the candidate speak for a greater portion of the time (they ought to talk for around 70 per cent of the time);
❑ listening actively;
❑ asking appropriate questions;
❑ avoiding stress;
❑ avoiding showing the candidates that they are wrong – the panel should remain neutral (p 113).

The tension and stress need to be minimised as much as possible, and one way of doing this is to have organised the interview so that the following is known:

❑ who will ask what questions;
❑ how the candidate will be welcomed;
❑ where they will wait;

❏   who will lead the panel;
❏   how long the interview will last;
❏   how the successful and unsuccessful candidates will be told the
     outcome of the interview.

Table 3.1 suggests some useful dos and don'ts. They are suggested by, but
abbreviated from, Everard and Morris, *Effective School Management* (1985).

Induction of a new member of staff

Most schools make sure that any new member of staff has a mentor. This
applies whether the appointment is for a senior position of someone with
several years' experience or to a colleague who is in their first few years of
teaching. This is because any new place of work will have different routines,
structures and means of organisation. One of the keys to the mentor system
is not to choose someone because of their hierarchical position. This can
often cut across the notion of confidentiality, which is important and can
mean that a younger teacher will not ask simple questions of a senior teacher
because they will not want to give the impression that they are confused,
or don't know something that is relatively simple. During the first few
weeks there must be time for meetings where the mentor can discuss
important aspects of the school and the new colleague can talk, ask
questions and, where appropriate, use the mentor as a counsellor. Different
schools will face different issues and the range of teaching experiences will
raise different needs, but there will usually be a broad range of written
documentation such as staff handbooks, for example. Brand (1993) in 'The
first week and how to survive it' raises important issues, as well as
reminding us all that the induction process should be about information
and not indoctrination. Schools do have managed routines and they do
have to maintain overall structures but within them, if the recruitment
process is effective, there will be a mix of new and old teachers with
individual strengths and beliefs. She goes on to say:

> I felt strong enough not to let myself slip into established ways just
> because they were there. I refused to abandon what I knew were good
> methods and to teach in a manner which went against all the reasons
> that I had entered the profession. Throughout the year I was supported
> by colleagues in many ways. I visited other schools, colleagues'
> classrooms and the deputy head taught in mine. I watched, listened,
> learned and I hope taught colleagues something new occasionally.
> (1993: 59)

Table 3.1 *Dos and don'ts of interviewing*

Do not:	❑ start with intimate, personal or argumentative questions;
	❑ use closed questions which will lead to a yes or no answer unless there is a need to establish a clear and specific fact;
	❑ use loaded questions, trick questions or jargon;
	❑ lead (the interviewee); for example 'I suppose you. . .', 'no doubt you enjoy good relations with. . .';
	❑ indicate disapproval or show that you are shocked;
	❑ worry about silences.
Do:	❑ use open ended questions which allow the candidates to express themselves and to demonstrate knowledge;
	❑ probe tactfully using 'why?', 'what?', 'how' questions or: 'tell me about. . .', 'what did you enjoy most about. . .?', 'what was your role in. . .?';
	❑ reassure a nervous candidate by smiling and making relaxing small talk;
	❑ listen for at least two-thirds of the time;
	❑ guide the candidate tactfully into the areas you wish to explore;
	❑ close down one area and open up another with remarks such as: 'ok. I think we have covered that; now could you tell me about. . .?';
	❑ come back to areas a candidate tries to avoid;
	❑ get his or her views on the job and invite views on the school;
	❑ observe behaviour such as nervousness, aggression and signs of stress;
	❑ when the candidate has had time to 'settle down' in the interview, look for clues for 'difficult adjustments' at previous schools (the inability to relate well to other people is the most frequent cause of disaffection with staff members of all kinds);
	❑ beware of your own prejudices, eg accent, dress, men with beards, women with earrings etc;
	❑ give the candidate a chance to ask about the job and check whether they have any reservations;
	❑ make sure that the interview panel has a few minutes to note overall impressions of one candidate before they begin interviewing the next.

There are two important points to make from Brand's article. First of all, she is suggesting that the school is supporting her and, secondly, that she is retaining her own sense of individuality within the parameters, structures and processes of the school. They are both essential. If we select the right person for the job we should expect them to bring their own flair and individualism with them. If they didn't then the school would be much less effective because there would be much less change and much slower growth and development.

DEVELOPING THE ROLE OF CURRICULUM COORDINATORS

Headteachers can't do everything. They have to delegate and manage the school through and with other people. Delegation involves the concepts of hierarchy, power, authority and responsibility. The headteacher who delegates is invariably in a position of power and by delegating you are giving some of that power to someone else. It is also important to be able to trust the colleague who has been given a job to do. In other words, delegation isn't just a random event, it is about choosing the right person for the job. Most delegation in primary schools is given to subject coordinators, and their link with an effective curriculum is the subject of Chapter 8. Before we look more specifically at some of their tasks it is important to recognise some broader issues. It is reasonable, for example, that:

❑ jobs that are delegated to coordinators are matched to individual strengths;
❑ the individuals who are given jobs are actually capable of doing them;
❑ once delegated, the coordinator has overall ownership of the tasks;
❑ in leading and managing change in a specific subject the coordinator will have to plan, support and monitor the innovation process.

Duties and roles of curriculum coordinators

As a headteacher, it is important to endorse the position of curriculum coordinators and to invest them with the power to do a specific job. Their role as manager, leader, change agent and, of course, coordinator will be in a position to be developed if they are known to be all these things and are not just seen as mouth pieces for the headteacher. Their role is complicated. Dean, in *Managing the Primary School* (1987), suggests that their managerial roles and duties include the following:

❏ supporting colleagues in their particular area of the curriculum;
❏ overseeing the subject content and the processes and teaching styles which are used in the classroom;
❏ preparing schemes of work;
❏ working with colleagues to select appropriate resources;
❏ inducting new colleagues into the work of the school in their subject;
❏ ensuring that adequate records are kept;
❏ advising the head on the specialist needs of the subject area.

Leadership and the curriculum coordinator

Most of the tasks suggested by Dean involve leadership of some kind and this is the subject of Chapter 6. If the leadership of a particular subject, however, is delegated to a specific person, they need to have the power and authority to lead. One of the key managerial and leadership roles for the coordinator is that of implementation. Change, and there has been a considerable amount, is extremely ineffective if it exists in limbo without being implemented. Once the change has reached schools, and recent innovations in literacy, numeracy and performance management are good examples, certain things have to happen. Those coordinators leading particular areas have to be persistent and have a sense of direction. Playfoot *et al* (1989) insist that 'the person leading the change needs to be visible, working with their sleeves rolled up, touring, talking, making practical adjustments, listening and leading on the job' (1989: 73).

Implementation, and those roles involving leadership and change, need energy, time and the commitment and ability to work with other people. Some of the characteristics of all leaders including curriculum coordinators will include:

❏ **self-awareness** – being aware of our own attitudes and values and how they affect other people;
❏ **the will to achieve** – seeking new challenges;
❏ **optimism** – feeling positive about the future and the part to be played in it;
❏ **positive regard** – responding to others with warmth and respect;
❏ **trust** – the extent we are prepared to trust colleagues;
❏ **congruence** – the security to work with colleagues;
❏ **empathy** – understanding colleagues' points of view;
❏ **courage** – taking risks to find other ways of working with colleagues.

Curriculum coordinators and time to do their job

One common complaint heard from all curriculum coordinators is that they have certain tasks to do and yet they have no time to do them. Nearly all primary teachers teach full time and very few are released from the classroom for tasks other than actual teaching. This is in many ways inevitable given the present funding of primary schools where even the most limited of release time is unavailable to even the most creative headteacher. This way of working, however, is self-defeating, because if a subject coordinator has certain tasks to complete they will be very frustrated if they are unable to complete them.

Everyone will be familiar with a teacher's professional duties which fit into what is known as directed time. This is the time allocated by the headteacher for the working day, week and ultimately year. There are certain tasks that a subject coordinator will have to fit into that time. Table 3.2 lists those tasks that will have to be completed within that ever-expanding amount of time that teachers spend working either in school or at home. Having said that, it will be obvious that many of the tasks are not new. They have always been part of the 'working day'. It is equally true, however, that for literacy and numeracy coordinators, for example, their work load has increased dramatically.

It is obvious from Table 3.2 that there is a formidable list of tasks to complete, plan and teach across the curriculum in the primary classroom. The increase in standards fund grants and a more creative use of the school budget have meant that many successful schools have realised the impossibility of trying to raise standards without releasing teachers from the classroom on a regular basis. Table 3.3 lists tasks that can only be completed by a coordinator when they are not teaching. In many ways it is a 'new' list but there are some similarities with Table 3.2 and it is to be hoped that some of the tasks listed in Table 3.2 could also be completed during time out of the classroom. What is important to recognise, however, is that the tasks listed in Table 3.3 largely depend on the coordinator working with or alongside colleagues.

What are your curriculum coordinators doing?

Working as a curriculum coordinator is difficult. There is little point in complaining that it is difficult without developing strategies to make it more effective in the time available. There is little point in creating yet another layer of monitoring or another pro forma to check what has been completed. The School Development Plan and the performance management reviews

Table 3.2 *Tasks to be completed in directed time*

A knowledge and understanding of:	❏ how their subject relates to the whole curriculum; ❏ the statutory national curriculum requirements; ❏ what high-quality teaching in their subject actually is; ❏ how this teaching will raise standards; ❏ all the evidence in the school and from external tests that will show what the school's levels of attainment and standards are; ❏ how to set targets for children in their subject.
The skills to:	❏ prioritise, plan and organise; ❏ work as part of a team or lead a team; ❏ secure a consistent approach throughout the school; ❏ use the expertise of other teachers; ❏ provide a role model; ❏ delegate tasks as appropriate; ❏ make judgements as to when to take decisions, when to consult and when to defer to senior teachers and the headteacher; ❏ understand data about levels of attainment; ❏ solve problems and identify new opportunities to raise standards; ❏ communicate effectively within school and with parents and inspectors and governors; ❏ chair meetings where appropriate.
Develop the subject by:	❏ writing and implementing policies; ❏ setting challenging targets for improvement; ❏ writing and implementing schemes of work; ❏ evaluating and monitoring policies and schemes of work.
Manage effective teaching and learning by:	❏ ensuring a consistent method of curriculum planning in the long, medium and short term; ❏ monitoring the planning in the medium and short term; ❏ making sure that teachers are aware of learning objectives and that these are made clear to the children;

Table 3.2 *(Contd)*

	❏ providing guidance on appropriate teaching and learning methods;
	❏ establishing policies for assessing, reporting and recording achievement.
Use resources effectively by:	❏ identifying appropriate resources;
	❏ ensuring that they are available for use fairly and safely;
	❏ establishing future resource needs and likely priorities for expenditure;
	❏ maintaining existing resources.
Continue with professional development by:	❏ attending appropriate courses;
	❏ feeding back relevant information to colleagues;
	❏ holding appropriate meetings to discuss relevant aspects of their subject;
	❏ taking part in training days by training colleagues in appropriate aspects of their subject.

Table 3.3 *Tasks to be completed during time outside the classroom*

❏ observing teachers in a consistent way (following the model of classroom observation used in performance management);
❏ feeding back to teachers in a constructive way about the quality of lessons in their subject;
❏ demonstrating good practice and teaching lessons with other colleagues observing;
❏ offering support in lessons by working alongside colleagues;
❏ observing lessons to identify children who should be targeted for SEN (or who are gifted and talented);
❏ working with children with SEN to improve their skills;
❏ training teaching assistants by working alongside them in classrooms;
❏ attending courses to improve subject skills;
❏ taking part in appropriate performance management meetings.

will identify what needs to be completed and when. It is then up to senior teachers and the headteacher to monitor the targets that have been set. Table 3.4 is a check list of questions to ask that will help headteachers focus on the areas that they need to develop most effectively both during their directed time and during their non-contact time.

Table 3.4 *Questions to ask curriculum coordinators*

❏ How do you influence the work of other teachers?
❏ Do you monitor, evaluate and feed back your views on medium- and short-term planning?
❏ Are you able to take part in joint planning with other teachers?
❏ Are you able to observe lessons and feed back on their quality?
❏ Do you work alongside teachers in their classrooms?
❏ How do you get an overview of the standards in your subject throughout the school?
❏ Do you regularly update the policies and scheme of work?
❏ Is there a consistent method of assessing and recording in your subject?
❏ What arrangements are there for SEN support in your subject?
❏ Are you in control of a budget for your subject?
❏ How do you identify what resources are needed?
❏ Where are resources stored and is there easy access?
❏ What training have you had in the past two years?
❏ Are appropriate targets set during performance management that relate to the School Development Plan?
❏ Do you train other staff?

DEVELOPING AND MANAGING EFFECTIVE TEAMS

At the beginning of the previous section it was made clear that the headteacher cannot do everything. It is also true to say that neither can individual coordinators. The headteacher can lead and develop the school and the coordinators can lead developments in their subject but they will not be able to improve the school and raise standards in particular areas without working with other people.

Charles Handy, in *Understanding Organisations* (1976), suggests several reasons why organisations use groups or teams of people rather than individuals. He includes:

❏ *for the distribution of work* – to bring together a set of skills, talents and responsibilities and allocate them their particular duties;
❏ *for the management and control of work* – to allow work to be organised and controlled by appropriate individuals with responsibility for a certain range of work;

❏ *for problem solving and decision taking* – to bring together a set of skills, talents and responsibilities so that the solution to any problem will have all available capacities applied to it;

❏ *for information processing* – to pass on decisions or information to all those who need to know;

❏ *for information and idea collection* – to gather ideas, information or suggestions;

❏ *for testing and ratifying decisions* – to test the validity of a decision taken outside the group or to ratify such a decision;

❏ *for coordination and liaison* – to coordinate problems and tasks between functions or divisions;

❏ *for increased commitment and involvement* – to allow and encourage individuals to get involved in the plans and activities of the organisation;

❏ *for negotiation and conflict resolution* – to resolve a dispute or argument (pp 155–56).

Teamwork is an excellent way of getting things done effectively. Team building, therefore, should form an important part of the headteacher's management function. If we accept Handy's main recommendations, a school without teams of teachers working together would be far less effective when taking decisions than one with a structure which values teams of teachers.

Individuals and teams

In response to the increasing amount of change, schools have created many different teams. Unfortunately, teams are made up of individuals and the effectiveness of such teams depends to a large extent on how well they can work together. On the other hand, the magnitude of educational change has been such that teams working together has been essential. Successful groups and teams produce better ideas in that the ideas themselves are better evaluated and thought through and they usually produce better solutions. Another way of recognising some of the problems associated with the formation of successful teams is to look at the stages of development that individuals have to go through before they begin to work together effectively (Table 3.5). These aspects of the formation of teams and groups are discussed in Handy, *Understanding Organisations* (1976: 171) and Smith, *Successful School Management* (1995, pp 12–13).

Managing and leading teams of teachers so that they reach stage 4 and perform is not easy. There are all kinds of problems with colleagues who aren't particularly involved in the task, who don't contribute in any positive

Table 3.5 *How groups form*

1. The group *forms*	This is the stage where individuals get together around one person who acts as a leader to solve a common problem or reach a decision about an important issue. At this stage most group members are anxious and over-dependent on the leader. This is a period of testing the water, as no one is quite sure what behaviour is acceptable. Each group member will be trying to find out what their task is, how they are going to go about it and what the expected outcome will be.
2. The group *storms*	This stage is common to all groups and occurs when members of the team do not agree. There is usually some kind of conflict between sub-groups within the team and sometimes rebellion against the leader. There is often resistance by individuals to being controlled and it is as if each member has to assert their individuality in some way. There is also resistance to getting on with the task in hand and most group members at this stage will feel that the task has no interest for them.
3. The group *norms*	This is where a more cohesive pattern of behaviour emerges. Resistance is overcome and conflicts are largely resolved because there is a feeling of mutual support. At this stage there will be open exchanges of views and a considerable amount of cooperation in trying to reach sensible and valuable conclusions.
4. The group *performs*	At this stage the group is beginning to achieve its outcomes and there are few interpersonal problems. Members know each other well and the group is able to move forward effectively. Solutions and outcomes emerge and there will be a constructive attempt to complete tasks efficiently.

way and whose personalities clash with other members of the team. This will inevitably mean that tension and often acrimonious exchanges will limit the effectiveness of the group. Because the four stages are common to most teams and groups, it is important that stage 4 is reached because it is only at this stage that there will be any useful outcomes from the group. The leader will often have to overcome all kinds of individual quirks and prejudices so that acceptable decisions that will move the school forward are actually taken. This will mean acting both assertively and decisively.

Managing the group or team to stage four is, unfortunately, not the end of the process. If important changes have been organised and/or decisions that will affect the way things happen have been taken, there will still be stormy waters to sail through because change is often difficult. This will mean being able to recognise some of the various characteristics of colleagues in the school so that it is possible to begin to understand the mix of individuals that make up the team, or in many primary schools make up all the staff.

Managing colleagues by understanding their characteristics

All teaching colleagues in your school are managers in some way and it is the headteacher's role to make sure that each individual is set targets that they can achieve and which will move the school forward. Groups working together, and this can mean the whole staff of a small school, are only successful and effective if they produce the appropriate results. Knowing who participates, who is negative to new proposals, who doesn't take part etc is vital to the success of how the school raises standards. Some of the characteristics that affect success will include:

❑ **Colleagues who always contribute** – It is useful to know who gets involved in discussions and participates a lot. It is equally important to know who sits back and leaves the talking to everyone else, even though you know that they have useful things to say. All colleagues need to contribute and need to participate. If they don't then the group may well under-perform and decisions taken will not be as effective as those taken when everyone participates.

❑ **Colleagues who influence others** – Some people who talk a lot and always contribute to meetings aren't always listened to. It is sometimes the case that quiet colleagues who contribute little are able to hold the attention of a meeting and say things that change the course of a decision. It is important to manage the whole area of 'influence' carefully because it may well be the case that some colleagues may have their own personal agendas which will not necessarily be the same as that of the school.

❏ **Influence that is either positive or negative** – There are colleagues in any school who are able to enlist the cooperation of others and those who always seem to alienate those they work with. An effective manager is able to detect these shifts of influence and balance the positive and negative colleagues appropriately. Some examples of the kinds of colleagues who will cause the most problems include:
   – *autocratic* colleagues who tell other people what to do and assume that their way is the only way;
   – *supporters* who agree with everything just to avoid conflict;
   – *distancers* who pretend that what is happening has nothing to do with them;
   – *judgemental* colleagues who belittle the views of colleagues by passing judgements that they assume are perfect and then block any movement in directions that they do not want to go;
   – *the democrat* who wants everyone to agree with everything and slows down the pace of change.

❏ **The effects of decision making** – Taking decisions will affect individual colleagues. If decisions are imposed, there will be those who disagree and are resentful that they have not been consulted. If the decision is shared, you still can't win because there will still be colleagues who think that their point of view is more important than the views of other colleagues. Consensus, while difficult to achieve, is one of the best ways of reducing the stress of new decisions and their inevitable change.

❏ **Continuing to work together** – Some colleagues are good at drawing people into discussions, listening to their points of view and generally making them feel valued. This doesn't always mean agreeing with them and it can mean rejecting their views. This has to happen, without demoralising colleagues and losing their support. Being able to do this is essential if moving things forward is a continuing rather than a one-off process.

❏ **Creating the right atmosphere** – This is very subjective, but it is common sense to assume that certain characteristics of a group of people working together will be more successful than others. Friendly, congenial, calm, tolerant, supportive are all words that suggest that groups where their members exhibit such traits are likely to be more successful than groups who don't. If such traits exist within meetings that are businesslike they should be very effective in making decisions that are appropriate and will be successfully carried out.

❏ **Belonging to the group** – It is essential that headteachers are able to manage staff in a way that prevents counterproductive and negative sub-groups forming that do not have the interests of the school and the development plan at heart. An atmosphere of an 'in' group and those who are 'out' is not conducive to raising standards.

Assertion and working with colleagues

It seems to me that all schools need high-quality teachers who are able to be part of the school's continuous debate about what needs to happen to raise standards. Rather than colleagues being too aggressive or too timid, schools need teachers and teaching assistants who are able to be assertive. This will not result in colleagues who are stroppy and argumentative but informed, decisive teachers who are able to be part of all the moves that are necessary in meeting targets and completing the objectives of the school development plan. Teachers who are either aggressive or timid are not really taking responsibility for their professional behaviour because timidity implies being easily manipulated and aggression tends to make colleagues feel undervalued and worthless.

Rowland and Birkett in *Personal Effectiveness for Teachers* (1992) see assertiveness as the key to managing schools more effectively for both headteachers and teachers who are subject coordinators. They suggest that:

> Being assertive means. . . having respect for ourselves and others, and being honest. It allows us to say what we want and feel but not at other people's expense. It means understanding the point of view of other people, and being self-confident and positive. It is not about winning come what may or getting your own way all the time. Assertiveness is about handling conflict and coming to an acceptable compromise. (1992: 6)

Rowland and Birkett suggest that all teachers should have the right to:

❏ have and express feelings and opinions;
❏ be listened to and taken seriously;
❏ set priorities;
❏ say 'no' without feeling guilty;
❏ ask for what they want;
❏ ask for and get information from each other;
❏ sometimes make mistakes.

If we accept that assertiveness is one of the keys to an effective school then we have to accept that there are times when everyone from the headteacher to the NQT has to be assertive. This does not always come naturally, and changing aggression or timidity to assertion is fraught with difficulties. Smith (1993), in *Preparing for Appraisal: Self Evaluation for Teachers in Primary and Secondary Schools*, suggests a step by step guide that teaches you how to be assertive, the assumption being that it is important and that in schools it is useful in situations when someone is asking you to do something that you are either unable to do because it is inconvenient in terms of time or short notice or that you don't want to do at all because you do not consider it to be part of your job. Table 3.6 suggests the kind of dialogue that can be learnt and the responses that need to be made in a specific order. The dialogue is based on the following scenario and is geared towards you as a headteacher teaching colleagues how to be assertive (it is assumed that all headteachers are already pretty assertive!): You receive a note from the headteacher telling you that because they are unable to attend a particular meeting you will have to go instead. However, you also cannot go at short notice because of prior commitments.

Table 3.6 *Step by step guide to assertion*

Step 1	*Summarise* the situation fairly, factually, carefully and straightforwardly. You could say: 'I am concerned that you have asked me to go to this meeting and I am not able to do so'.
Step 2	*State how you are feeling about it.* This is how you feel, not how anyone else feels. You could say: 'I am concerned that although it is important, I am just not available to go'.
Step 3	*Describe why you cannot go,* why you feel concerned and why you are unable to respond in the way that is wanted. You might say: 'I have already arranged a brief meeting with Mrs X and then I am expected home because of a long-standing theatre commitment'.
Step 4	*Empathise with your colleague's point of view or the position they are in.* You can suggest: 'I can understand the need for someone to go to the meeting but I already have a busy schedule for that evening'.
Step 5	*Specify what you think should happen.* It is important not to be totally negative, but to try to find a solution or compromise. For example, you could say: 'If it is not really possible for any of us to be there, I will telephone a colleague in another school who should be going and ask her to collect all the information she can and we can collect it at the end of the week'.
Step 6	*Take decisions about what you final response will be.* This should not threaten the other person. You could say: 'I think that my solution could work reasonably well. I am sorry that I cannot go but, as I have already said, I have already made other arrangements'.

I'M OK, ARE YOU OK?

In this final section of the chapter we need to think in simple terms about how best to work with colleagues. A successful manager will get the best out of people. Working together as a cohesive team is one of the keys to a successful school. So, in its simplest terms, the OK colleague is easy to work with and will be cooperative and responsive. Unfortunately, we all have to work alongside not-OK colleagues who are relatively unresponsive. Montgomery (1989) in *Managing Behaviour Problems* takes the OK and not-OK analogy a step further and produces a useful summary of what she sees as four positions that colleagues can be in and which will need managing in different ways:

❏ *Position 1 is I'm OK, you're also OK* – This means that everyone is working well together and the management of change as well as decision making is relatively easy and straightforward.
❏ *Position 2 is I'm OK, but you are far from OK* – This is mainly about the selfish manager or leader in a situation getting their own way. It is not really the position for working together and any decisions taken will be admired by the minority and resented by the majority.
❏ *Position 3 is I'm not OK, but you are OK* – This is the position where there is an isolated group who see themselves as underachieving while everyone else seems to be achieving something and being far more successful.
❏ *Position 4 is where I'm not OK and you're not OK either* – If this is the situation in your school then you are managing a group of people, none of whom feel that they are actually getting anywhere. This is obviously an intolerable position where no decisions are taken that can possibly work and lead to any worthwhile change.

Both you and all your colleagues need to feel that they are playing a productive part in the school. *Position 1* is the ideal position that has to be aimed for. If this is not the position you are at, then those who manage will have to make sure that the relationships are mended and may well have to assert their views and beliefs so that confidence will return and the jobs that have to be done are dealt with effectively.

IMPORTANT POINTS

The key points made in this chapter have centred round the concepts of recruiting staff and making sure that they can work together to produce the kind of results that raise standards:

❏ There needs to be an effective recruitment policy.
❏ The whole process has to begin with an appropriate job description for the post that is advertised and end with an interview that will ask the kind of questions that will identify the best candidate.
❏ Once a teacher is appointed, it is more than likely that they will have to take on the role of curriculum coordinator. An effective head will delegate tasks to all teachers.
❏ These tasks will relate to the performance management review and will involve the coordinator playing their part as leaders of specific areas of the curriculum.
❏ Many of their tasks will have to be completed within the statutory hours of directed time.
❏ It is important, however, to realise that to do their jobs properly, coordinators will have to be released from the classroom and from their role as class teachers.
❏ If all primary teachers are coordinators, they are also all part of teams that need to work together.
❏ Headteachers need to be able to manage successful teams and know how individuals work together in the most effective ways.

THE SCHOOL AS AN ORGANISATION

In Chapters 1 and 2, a great deal was said about school ethos, the aims statement and the key planning that drives the school forward. This included the development plan, the curriculum plan and the plan for high-quality teaching and learning. The organisation of the school is largely about how these fit together and are effective through the people who work in the school. In Chapter 3 the key issues centred around how to recruit the right staff and how subject coordinators can be used to move the school forward.

How these elements are absorbed in the basic organisational structure of the school is extremely important. There has been a suggestion, and this will be followed up in the next chapter, that high burn-out schools with unacceptable levels of stress tend to have an autocratic management style that is geared wholly to academic achievement and clearly defined hierarchies, with individuals working alone rather than in teams. In low burn-out schools, and I would argue that these are the most effective schools, educational objectives are flexible, there is less pressure for high standards, although high standards are achieved, and there is an organisational structure where teachers meet in both large and small groups both to take decisions and to socialise.

THE MANAGEMENT STRUCTURE

Figure 4.1 illustrates the most usual management structure where the pyramid has the headteacher at the top in isolation and most teachers as a flat base. This does not rule out consultation or shared decision making, but it does assume a certain amount of 'us' and 'them' in the management structure. There will obviously be a senior management team and much consultation with teachers who will all have some kind of leadership and management role as curriculum and subject coordinators.

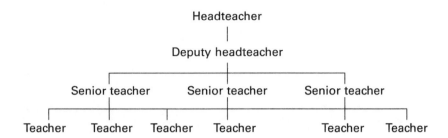

Figure 4.1 *Management structure*

The new pay and conditions of service introduced in September 2000 gives schools the opportunity to add to the leadership group of heads and deputies. This could flatten the top of the pyramid in Figure 4.1 slightly but, at the same time, increase the hierarchical division between those who manage and those who teach. It is important to recognise that those at the 'bottom' of the pyramid have the responsibility for raising achievement and there has to be a route within the organisation for them to influence how the school functions.

Results versus relationships

Any school has to be organised in such a way that there is a balance between high achievement and results and the maintenance of relationships, team building and results through training and developing staff. This will involve staff having three sets of needs that are able to shift and change in terms of which have priority. All three needs will affect the ethos as well as the organisation of the school and will include:

❏ the achievement of high test results and high attainment from all pupils;
❏ the professional needs of all staff;
❏ the needs of individual staff.

The results–relationship continuum in Figure 4.2 will allow you to place the organisational structure of your school alongside it. The descriptions of each section of the continuum will also mean that you should consider whether you are where you would like to be or whether you would like to be in a different position. This aspect of school organisation is important because it can affect the ethos of the school. If you want a certain ethos but find that the type of organisation makes this difficult, you will have to consider what changes are possible and necessary.

Figure 4.2 *The results–relationship continuum*

The points on the continuum are as follows:

❏ **Autocratic** – At this end of the continuum the strategy for organising the school is largely dependent on *'telling'*. Orders are given and they are expected to be followed.
❏ **Paternalistic** – This stage means that a certain amount of dialogue will be part of the organisation. Colleagues will be expected to talk to each other and there will be an attempt to *'sell'* ideas by persuasion. The discussions that take place will not really go beyond agreeing with the ideas that are being put forward.
❏ **Consultative** – This will mean that *'involving'* colleagues becomes part of the organisational culture of the school. Staff will be consulted about new ideas, changes in direction and new or different ways of working. This will mean that the organisation moves towards a more collegial structure.
❏ **Democratic/collegial** – At this end of the continuum, the management processes which govern how the school's ethos and aims develop must involve consensus and recognise that colleagues, who all have delegated responsibilities, must be able to 'share and co-determine' what happens in the school. This type of organisation involves many working teams and a considerable number of meetings.

Basic organisational concepts

I have already mentioned *Understanding Organisations* by Charles Handy (1976). It is an important book for anyone interested in how organisations work. Many of the business and industry theories used by Handy and others can be applied to schools. Some of them will include the following, which I have linked to other chapters and, rather than offer detailed explanations, I have asked questions which can be applied to any schools. By asking the most appropriate questions of your school you will be able to understand more about how it is organised.

Setting objectives

This is really about the aims of the organisation, what it intends to do and what its expectations are. Schools, of course, are about teaching and learning and any strategies that the school uses will be of interest to both parents and governors and need to be shared with them:

❑ What is the school planning to do in the future?
❑ What are its expectations in terms of raising standards, developing staff etc?
❑ How are the school's objectives shared with parents, governors and any other outside agencies?

The structure of the school

The hierarchical pyramid and the results–relationship continuum are about how the school is structured to make it work. Primary schools have all kinds of structures in place. They include groupings of children into classes, staffing teams, teams of teaching assistants etc:

❑ What are the roles and tasks of each teacher?
❑ How is change managed?
❑ Who takes decisions and how?
❑ Who works alongside whom and why?

Leadership and power

Most teachers have to lead and if, for example, they are coordinators of numeracy and literacy they will need considerable leadership skills. It is also the case that both formal and informal power is in the hands of different people:

❑ Who are leaders and who is allowed and expected to lead?
❑ Who takes hold of a new initiative and moves things forward?
❑ Who is willing to take responsibility for new change and development?
❑ Who is given the authority to move the school forward?
❑ Who is able to use their power and authority positively?
❑ Who uses their authority in a negative way?

Culture

This is synonymous with ethos and, like the ethos of the school, is determined by the school's beliefs and values. It is a combination of the social, moral and academic values of the school and is basically about how the people that work in the organisation relate to each other and to the children they teach. What the culture or ethos is will rely on such concepts as courtesy, care, consideration, competition, individuality as well as what is considered right and proper:

❏ What are the core values of your school?
❏ What are the beliefs that determine your academic curriculum?

External relationships

No school exists on its own in a kind of educational vacuum. All schools are part of a wider environment and a broader context. This may be, quite simply, the kind of school you work in, for example Infant, Junior, Primary, Catholic or Church of England. The catchment area will also influence the organisational structure of the school. For example, a small rural school will present different challenges from those of a large urban school. School governors are perhaps the most important external group of people who need to be involved in the school's organisation. Their expectations, involvement and ambitions for the school will influence many of its.

Organisational structures within the school

There are close links and a certain amount of interdependency between internal and external influences on how a primary school is organised. Table 4.1 attempts to link some of the issues.

Class groupings will be partly dependent on the number of children on the school's roll and the number of teachers paid on management scales will be closely linked to the amount of money available in the school budget. The budget itself, of course, is also largely dependent on the number of children on roll, and subject coordination and room allocation will be affected by the number of teachers, the number of children and the length of the school day.

All this implies that how the school is organised will be dependent on the interrelationship of different structures as well as the balance between the individual and the organisation. Table 4.2 identifies the kind of movement that has to happen across the organisation.

Table 4.1 *Internal and external structures*

INTERNAL STRUCTURES	EXTERNAL STRUCTURES
Class groupings	Numbers on roll
Registration groups	Admission numbers
Subject groups	Salary scales
Subject groups	School budget
Year teams	Leaving ages
Departments	Statutory length of the school day
Responsibility allowances	Members of the governing body
Timetables and room allocations	New central initiatives such as:
Meetings	❏ Literacy
Committees	❏ Numeracy
Working parties etc	❏ Performance management

Table 4.2 *The individual, the group and the organisation*

INDIVIDUAL	GROUP	WHOLE ORGANISATION
Head	Classes	Nursery
Deputy	Years	Infant
Senior teachers	Key stages	Junior
Coordinators/teachers	Working groups and teams	
Parents	Planning teams	
Governors	Key stage teams	
Site manager	Curriculum teams	
Secretary/bursar etc		

The school cannot function without working teams of teachers. Teams cannot function without their individual members and single teachers cannot perform all their functions without being part of a decision-making team. The link between the individual, the group and the organisation could be extended to include a wider network of influential groups, including LEAs, teacher unions and the DfEE. But however far we extend these aspects of the organisation and the influences on it, we cannot and must not lose sight of the fact that its effectiveness will depend on individuals working together to raise standards and achieve success within the individual school.

Working with governors

Schools cannot and should not try to function as an organisation without involving governors. There are two key areas where they can function effectively and help take decisions that will not only make the school more effective but will enable them to be more supportive. The two key areas that need to be well organised are the curriculum and the inspection process. Both areas are the subject of separate chapters, but this section is from the governor's perspective. Before looking at these two areas, let's briefly summarise some other governor–school issues.

People's perceptions of what happens in school are almost as important as what actually does happen. Governors are able to bring the perceptions of business and the local community, and it is vital that their understanding of what goes on is as full and as accurate as possible. There are two ways of doing this: informally and formally.

❑ Involving governors informally – Examples of informal governor involvement will include:
  – PTA functions such as school fetes, quizzes, dances etc;
  – school plays, concerts, parties etc;
  – retirement functions for staff, presentations, end of term dinners;
  – general meetings with parent governors in and around school as they take their children to classes.
❑ Examples of formal involvement include:
  – full governors' meetings which are usually held twice each term;
  – subcommittee meetings such as curriculum, finance, premises etc;
  – staff appointments and interviews;
  – arrangements to visit the school and work with teachers or watch lessons;
  – headteacher's performance management;
  – Ofsted inspection process where governors are required to talk to the inspectors.

(It is important that on formal occasions you are well briefed, clear about your views on specific issues and aware of the kinds of perspectives that the governors are bringing to each meeting.)

The informal functions should be relaxed occasions where governors are able to meet with staff, parents, children and other members of the community. As well as the functions listed, it is also a good idea if the headteacher and chair of governors and the headteacher and chair of finance are able to meet relatively informally each term as well as at formal governors' meetings. Doing this will give more opportunities for relationships to be deepened on the basis of mutual trust and respect.

On both formal and informal occasions, governors will have the opportunity to gain insights about the school and to make contributions to the life of the school.

GOVERNORS AND THE CURRICULUM

The governors, together with the headteacher, are responsible for making sure that the National Curriculum and its assessment procedures are carried out properly. They cannot possibly take on this responsibility, albeit through the quality of the headteacher's leadership and organisational skills, without knowing a considerable amount about what it is that they are responsible for. There are many ways in which governors can be kept informed about the curriculum. They will include:

❏ making sure that the headteacher's report has a section on the curriculum at certain times of each year;
❏ setting up a committee specifically for curriculum issues;
❏ at governors' meetings, or at curriculum committee meetings, having specific curriculum coordinators to talk to governors;
❏ inviting governors to share training days and/or sharing training on important curriculum issues;
❏ making sure that the governors are involved in the writing and approval of all curriculum policies;
❏ involving governors in school development planning;
❏ allowing governors to visit classes and see the curriculum in action;
❏ reporting the results of national tests and discussing the implications and analysis of them;
❏ identifying with governors the strengths and weaknesses of how the school interprets and delivers the curriculum in terms of quality and raising standards.

Of course, these initiatives will only work well if there is a relationship and ethos which makes governors feel valued by teachers. Their knowledge and their feelings of being worth consulting on professional issues will put them in a much stronger position when it comes to responding to parental queries, talking to inspectors and representing the school in other LEA meetings.

Governors and their responsibilities

Let's start by reminding ourselves what the governors' responsibilities are in relation to the curriculum. They need to make sure that the following is happening:

❏ The National Curriculum is being taught in full.
❏ Religious education is taught.
❏ The school's national assessment results are sent to the LEA each year.
❏ The sex education policy is approved each year.
❏ There is a written policy on the curriculum (this is not a statutory requirement).

This may look relatively simple but it does in fact include all the most important things the school does and, of course, makes it a large and difficult job. The job is so large, in fact, that governing bodies will appreciate all the professional advice and experience that the headteacher and teachers can give. This doesn't mean any loss of authority on the headteacher's part or any removal of the head's statutory responsibilities. Table 4.3 suggests ways in which the head, with the support of his or her staff, can help the governors through their obligations.

How governors can be involved in curriculum policies

One of the most important areas of school organisation is the development planning cycle, which culminates in the current School Development Plan and begins the next cycle of planning. The organisation of this process means that the headteacher has to make sure that there is a constant rolling programme of maintaining those areas that are working well and developing areas that are either new or that are scheduled to be changed as part of the cycle of development.

Let's imagine that the School Development Plan has identified that a certain policy document is several years old and needs modifying with a view to making radical changes. If your school's Maths and/or English policies were developed up to four years ago, for example, the introduction of the literacy and numeracy strategies will have meant the need for considerable change. It is also useful to consider an appropriate life span for policy statements and schemes of work. How long is it, for example, before there needs to be major changes as opposed to minor tinkering? Having identified the need for a new policy, there are several organisational steps that can be taken:

Table 4.3 *How to support governors*

1. Make sure you and your staff are as well informed as possible	The school has to offer advice to governors on the organisation of the school and the curriculum that is offered. It is not the other way round. This will mean that all staff need to know about the statutory requirements, any new changes and any possible future developments as well as what is in the Curriculum sections of the School Development Plan.
2. Plan ahead and get governors to plan ahead	This will mean not springing any surprises. All meetings should be scheduled well in advance, and minutes, reports and agendas circulated at appropriate times so that everyone has the right information for any discussions that might be needed.
3. Edit, summarise and précis	Governors have other jobs. You don't. This means that you shouldn't expect governors to read everything that you have to. They do need, however, to have the same information in a simpler, edited form which hasn't cut out the bits you don't want them to know.
4. Finding the information	It is possible to build up a library of information for governors with all the information they might need to read when they have time. They could also be reminded that the Internet has useful Web sites, such as that of the DfEE, which are a valuable source of information.
5. Getting the timing right	The chair of governors and the clerk to the governors should have a good idea about the pattern of the governors' year and what needs to be raised at particular meetings. It is also important that you look back over the previous year to find out, for example, the appropriate time for reviewing the sex education policy.
6. Governors have responsibilities	It is not the headteacher's responsibility, or part of his or her organisational skills, to manage the governors' meetings and activities. The

governors, usually through the chair, need to have particular responsibilities such as for literacy, numeracy and special educational needs. They also need to be part of the subcommittees that should exist for finance, curriculum, personnel and premises.

7. The headteacher's relationship with the chair of governors

It is important that there is a positive exchange of information with the chair. It is equally important that this is not seen as a relationship that takes most of the decisions that are then rubber-stamped by the full governing body. Regular meetings should be arranged and there should be consultation about the agenda for meetings so that appropriate tasks can be delegated to other governors and they can be consulted on what their subcommittees will be bringing to the meeting in terms of papers, handouts and reports.

8. The governors have a strategic responsibility

Don't expect everything to be rubber-stamped and be prepared to listen to what they say when they are presented with curriculum issues. There is no reason why they should have detailed curriculum documents, unless that is what they have asked for, but as part of their strategic responsibility, they need to know the principles so that they can offer reasoned advice and make sound decisions.

9. They need to visit the school

It is often difficult for governors who lead busy working lives to visit the school, but it is important to try to encourage them to come and see what is happening. It will make much more sense and focus attention for the short period of time available, if these visits are centred round a specific issue. For example, governors could look at writing lessons, or see how the new PE apparatus is being used, or watch an assembly and see if they can see whether it is of a broadly Christian nature and whether it encourages awe and wonder.

❏ It is part of the School Development Plan so it is flagged up to you, to other teachers and to governors who have their own copy of the SDP that change is needed. On the SDP will be who owns this task, the time span and the kinds of time in terms of meetings, training days etc that it is suggested are needed to make the changes.

❏ The governors' curriculum committee is told which policy it is that is being changed and possibly rewritten, and discussing a draft of the changed policy is put on the appropriate curriculum committee meeting agenda.

❏ The subject coordinator drafts a policy statement and consults widely in school during appropriate meetings.

❏ Staff comments are received and adopted as appropriate. The policy statement has to be in line with the school's aims and ethos and teachers will want to make sure that what it says will happen is realistic and can be made to happen.

❏ The draft is presented at the next governors' committee meeting. It is very effective if the subject coordinator is able to discuss the draft with the governors and they are given plenty of opportunity to discuss the policy and to find out what the implications are for its daily use in the classroom.

❏ It is at this curriculum subcommittee meeting that the draft receives its final corrections before it is passed back to teachers for any of their individual minor corrections, which, at this stage, will be limited to simple text changes, not changes to the substance of the policy.

❏ The draft is rewritten from the amendments and corrections and then presented at the full governors' meeting, which will pass the document because the curriculum committee will have fully approved it.

❏ The policy will be used in school to govern the content of what is taught and the processes of how a particular subject is taught. If there are staff development issues and training is needed, then this will be arranged, but this is not a responsibility of the governing body.

❏ This might seem to be a very lengthy and drawn-out process, and it has to be said that it can last for two terms, but it does provide opportunities for teachers and governors to feel involved in the development of important policy statements.

GOVERNORS AND THE INSPECTION PROCESS

There are now either long or short inspections. Short are for those schools that are already regarded as the most effective. This section is based on the procedures for long inspections, but most of it will be sound organisational practice which will apply to short inspections and other changes that might occur if there are further modifications to the whole Ofsted process. Chapter 9 will look more closely at the school's involvement in inspection but governors need to be prepared and they need to be able to demonstrate how well they perform their allocated duties and tasks. The emphasis in any inspection is on how children learn and teachers teach. Governors aren't observed in close detail but they are regarded as responsible for the way that the school is run.

As soon as notification is received that an inspection is imminent there will have to be a special governors' meeting arranged to discuss and plan what needs to happen before, during and after the inspection. If you have to panic and if the governors are totally unsure about what to do, when to do it and how, then there are problems that will have to be solved extremely quickly. Effective school organisation should mean that you, your staff and your governors are in a permanent state of readiness. The inspection is, after all, investigating everything that should be happening anyway. There shouldn't have to be a flurry of urgent activity just because there is an inspection, and you should discourage this kind of activity. By all means check carefully that the whole school reflects the ideal in terms of tidiness, wall displays etc. And by all means rush around tidying up and make sure all resources are where they should be; but having to write schemes of work and policies in a hurry is not the best kind of organisation to present to Ofsted inspectors. Apart from anything else, this kind of panic approach will leave everyone exhausted before the inspection even starts and will distract colleagues from planning 'perfect' lessons, which are the crucial matters of teaching and learning.

Telling the governors what to expect

It is important that during the pre-arranged governors' meeting there is a precise schedule of issues to be covered. Don't leave it to chance. The purpose of the meeting will be to:

❑ summarise the whole process for governors;
❑ make a list of times when governors are available during the inspection week to talk to inspectors;
❑ make sure that the clerk and the chair are aware that all their paperwork is up to date;
❑ tell parent governors what the parents' meeting will entail;
❑ try to arrange for as many governors as possible to be available to meet the registered inspectors when they make their first visit to the school;

❏ arrange the time and dates for the feedback meeting;
❏ make sure that they are aware of the timescales involved when the report is received, publishing the summary to parents, drawing up the action plan and sending it to all parents;
❏ take decisions about how to support staff during the inspection and what kind of stress-releasing event will be organised at the end of the inspection.

It is also extremely important to make sure that all the governors are aware of what exactly they are being measured against. This is quite clearly stated on pages 99–100 in *Inspecting Schools: Handbook for Inspecting Primary and Nursery Schools* (Ofsted, 1999):

1. 'The extent to which the governing body appraises the work of the headteacher and sets performance targets for him and her' (1999: 99).
2. 'Their knowledge of the strengths and weaknesses of the school and understanding of the challenges it faces' (1999: 100).
3. 'How well they have responded to the previous inspection' (1999:100).

Sharing the information that governors need

The chair of governors, chair of finance and probably the governors responsible for literacy, numeracy and special educational needs will all meet with inspectors at some time during the inspection week. It is a good idea to meet with each of these governors separately, together with the relevant subject coordinator, and talk through what is likely to happen, and where possible to pre-empt the kinds of questions that are going to be asked. It would be a mistake to find that there were contradictions in what the inspectors were being told. It is no good if the governors are saying that all decisions are taken by the school and the chair and yet you are saying that all the governors are fully involved in formulating policy decisions. Make sure that the terms of reference and all processes are up to date and widely understood. It will help if you make sure that everyone:

❏ understands the issues and avoids contradiction;
❏ has all the appropriate facts;
❏ has evidence that they know what is happening in school;
❏ knows a lot about their area of responsibility;
❏ knows what their statutory responsibilities are and is making sure that they are being met;
❏ is clear about why decisions are taken and what they hoped to achieve through them;

❏ understands the school's management structure and why it is arranged in the way that it is.

All this should not be too difficult if copies of all the recent minutes and documents are available and there is a history of the school sharing information with the governors. As well as current documents, of course, the last inspection report and the post-Ofsted Action Plans need to be clearly understood.

The governors' areas of responsibility

The new framework of inspection means that governors who are interviewed need to know about the school's strengths and weaknesses and how the school is being organised to raise standards. Much of the information that they need will be in the form of the School Development Plan and all governors will be expected to know what is in it. Table 4.4 suggests that as well as general issues, they are also likely to be asked about specific areas of responsibility.

There are, of course, certain statutory responsibilities that governors need to be aware of because any governor who is interviewed might be asked how they are met. For example, performance management and personnel governors will be asked about how these duties are organised in school.

Table 4.4 *Governors' specific areas of responsibility*

1. The chair of the finance committee	He or she will be expected to explain how the budget is allocated and how it is used to support the School Development Plan.
2. Literacy and numeracy governors	They will be expected to reflect on the implementation of their respective strategies and the impact on standards.
3. The SEN governor	He or she will need to know how much money the school spends on SEN, what provision the school makes for those children and the impact it has on their progress.
4. The chair of governors	He or she will need to talk about the way the school evaluates its own progress and development and how this information is used to move things forward.

Questions might centre around appointments and equal opportunities, staff development and the way performance management is related to raising standards and improving teachers' skills. In other words, they need to have an overview of these systems and procedures and need to have information that is up to date and accurate so that they can support and discuss the work of the school since the last inspection.

The organisation after the inspection

The first task is the meeting with the registered inspector for feedback about what the team has seen. This will be a summary of what will be in the report and it will present in a factual way the inspector's most important judgements and the key issues for action. The responsibilities now are to make sure that when the report is received by the school a summary is sent to parents, the post-inspection action plan is prepared and this is also sent to all parents.

In many ways, the inspection process is part of a cycle of change and improvement. It is a good idea to build in a period of calm and reflection after the inspection and then to begin the cycle of improvement that begins with implementing the post-inspection action plan and making sure that not only is the organisation of the school equipped to do this, but that the School Development Plan is also a visible and important part of the cycle.

COMMUNICATING THE SCHOOL'S AIMS TO PARENTS

Effective communication between home and school has to be actively promoted and the organisation of a shared partnership is important to teachers, children and parents. It is also about accountability and the relationships that are established between home and school. Many of the ways in which communication with parents are organised will be similar to those occurring within the school and will demand the same skills that are associated with meetings, face-to-face communication and written documents. What is important, however, is that these skills need to be geared to the specific audience. Parents do need information about what the school is trying to do in terms of raising standards but they don't need and nor should they expect a copy of the School Development Plan or the Curriculum policy.

There are four main ways to share information with parents about the school and about their children. They include:

❏ open evenings and written reports;
❏ governors' annual report to parents;
❏ school prospectus;
❏ regular newsletters and information.

Each school has to make its own decisions as to how parents will be involved in the school and the extent of the communication that takes place. These organisational decisions must take into account the school's need to receive feedback from parents as well as the need to develop an understanding of how parents view the school.

It is no good expecting feedback unless there are opportunities for this to take place. Annual written reports on children, for example, need a section for parent and child comments. The termly open evenings have to be a dialogue where effective teachers give their own findings on each individual child as well as making sure that they listen to the parent's view on how they feel their child is learning. Part of the Ofsted inspection process is to hold a meeting where parents are invited to tell the registered inspector what they think of the school in response to a series of questions. It is extremely useful to anticipate your next Ofsted inspection in order that you can send out a similar questionnaire, so that you have the answers in advance and can be seen to be doing something about the concerns well before Ofsted arrive.

The governors' annual report to parents and the statutory meeting that has to be held should be a useful forum for passing information to parents and listening to their concerns. Unfortunately, the written report often remains unread and many such meetings have more governors present than parents. One document that is read widely is the school prospectus which, if well organised and well presented, can be an excellent marketing tool for the school as well as a source of crucial information in summary about key issues such as the School Development Plan, SEN provision etc. It is worth looking in more detail at this document. It has to be said, however, that current legislation suggests that it must contain the following, although there have been frequent changes and, no doubt, there will be many more.

This summary includes both what has to be included and what should be included in order to give parents as much information as possible:

❏ admission arrangements;
❏ aggregate assessment results;
❏ the number of places available;
❏ practical details, eg school name, address etc, name of headteacher and chair of governors;
❏ dates of holidays for current year and times of school sessions;

❏ summary of charges and remissions policy;
❏ rates of unauthorised absences;
❏ details of arrangements of SEN children;
❏ complaints policy;
❏ sex education policy;
❏ details of RE and collective worship and a reminder that parents can withdraw children from such activities;
❏ statement on the organisation of the curriculum and teaching methods.

Parents can often be an under-used resource in the life of the school and organising them as a positive influence is not always easy. Schools communicate with parents as part of a two-way process, but many parents would also like the opportunity to help in school. There are at least three good reasons why the partnership with parents should be extended:

1. When this happens, they gain first-hand knowledge, first-hand experience and a degree of insight into how the school functions.
2. Parents working in school are able to offer a wide range of skills and interests that might otherwise not be available.
3. It is more than likely that they will become excellent public relations officers for the school and offer strong support for all the school's activities.

Table 4.5 summarises what needs to be shared with parents as well as the four areas of planned and organised development that can influence how successful the school is in sustaining an effective partnership.

ORGANISING THE BUDGET

Schools having their own budget has now been in place in one form or another since the early days of the Education Reform Act of 1988. LEAs have interpreted how finance is devolved to schools in different ways, so it is impossible to provide a definitive and detailed guide as to its effectiveness. There are, however, several key issues that are well worth raising and discussing.

The 1988 Act passed budgetary control from LEAs to individual schools and over a period of years this has been refined and perfected until now almost all funds are the school's responsibility. The major aims of redistributing the finance were: 1) to give greater flexibility in the spending of the budget; 2) to give schools the opportunity to respond more readily to the changing needs of its children and the local community.

Table 4.5 *What needs to be implemented and how*

All schools need to implement the following:	❏ Policy documents related to parents and their children, including a home–school partnership agreement, anti-bullying policy etc.
	❏ Details of all national test scores published and distributed in the school prospectus and governors' annual report to parents.
	❏ Informal visits to school should be relatively easy to organise.
	❏ Open evenings should be held each term.
	❏ Each child should have an annual written report.
	❏ Other meetings should include: PTA social events, meetings to explain curriculum issues to parents, induction meetings for new parents etc.
	❏ Regular newsletters from school and from parent governors.
	❏ Summaries of Ofsted reports, action plans etc.
How the partnership with parents will work best includes:	❏ *Teachers initiating action* – There is no point parents becoming involved in the school or being given piles of information unless the school knows what it wants from parents and how to summarise key issues. Heads need to ask their staff, governors and as many parents as possible, the following key questions: – How can we find out what parents want to know? – How can we use parents in school? – Have we got all the important methods of communicating with parents in place?
	❏ *Promoting communication and action* – If parents are going to help in school, they all need to be offered the opportunity, not just a select few who could provide the basis for cliques. Drawing up a list of activities needed and then matching them against the

Table 4.5 *(Contd)*

---

skills of parents is a useful way of making sure that opportunities are offered across the whole of the parental body.

❏ *Controlling what happens* – Both the headteacher and individual teachers who are working alongside volunteer parents must make it clear whether regular or occasional help is wanted and when it is required. Planned regular help should be the aim so that each teacher can communicate to parents what they will be doing and plan for the availability of an extra adult.

❏ *Maintaining the partnership* – Parents must feel welcome in the school and should be part of the team. This will mean that they work alongside specific teachers and also share breaks and refreshments. Teachers are in control and must both want parents working with them and be capable of planning for this to happen, so that parents are involved in any classroom activities without taking the teacher away from their first and most important commitment, which is to teach the children in the class.

Like many changes, the control schools now have over their budgets has become an accepted part of how the headteacher organises the school. But it has created pluses and minuses for all teachers who are involved in the management of schools. Table 4.6 identifies some of these positive and negative issues.

The budgeting process

There are many computer software systems that are used by LEAs and schools to make the monitoring of the budget easier. By 2004 all schools will have to produce financial statements to a common format.

The appropriate governors and the headteacher need to meet regularly to manage the budget and these meetings need to be carefully minuted

Table 4.6 *Management implications of the school budget*

POSITIVE ISSUES INCLUDE:	NEGATIVE ISSUES INCLUDE:
❏ Flexibility of spending. ❏ School able to identify its own priorities. ❏ Choice. ❏ Independence. ❏ More easily accountable. ❏ Opportunity to match funds to needs. ❏ Freedom from bureaucracy.	❏ Additional management tasks. ❏ Additional responsibility. ❏ Diversion of headteacher/ classroom time to management and accountancy. ❏ Formula funding can be arbitrary and not necessarily match the economic needs of the school. ❏ More meetings have to be held between the headteacher and the governors' chair of finance.

because it is public money that is being managed in schools. It is also useful to share information about the school's finance with teachers, especially the deputy head and senior teachers, because the School Development Plan will be matched against the budget and many of the tasks will have cost implications. It is also important because you will be looking for advice on current and future spending and if teachers are suddenly confronted with a question about finance that has never been raised before, they are less likely to provide you with advice that is helpful and relevant.

A budgeting sequence in a primary school might look like this (I have not included the kinds of meetings that will be required or tried to match the school year with the financial year):

❏ November
  – Start the process that identifies the numbers of children coming into school in September.
  – Work out the sizes of year groups and how many teachers and teaching assistants will be needed.
  – Look at the current SDP and check spending against tasks.
  – Look through a breakdown of spending and check over- and under-spends.
❏ January
  – Use potential year groups and class sizes to decide how many teachers and teaching assistants are needed.
  – Calculate spending needs on subject resources.
  – Go through staff development costs and prioritise future needs from

SDP and performance management targets.
- Keep working through current spending for over- and under-spends.
- Are there any areas where there will be a need for significant expenditure, eg you may want to suggest staff promotions, a change in status for the school bursar, more classroom assistants, more spending on literacy, ICT etc?

❏ February
- Indicative budgets, which should be similar to the final budgets, are sent to schools.
- Check through for mistakes, especially in terms of the right number of children being used for the budget calculations and the correct number of teachers and assistants etc.
- Work out draft spending and discuss implications with staff.
- Look at any standards fund grants and take decisions about how they should be spent. . . always bearing in mind the School Development Plan and those areas identified as priorities for raising standards.

❏ March
- Set the budget.
- Explain to everyone who has a stake in the budget what the positive and negative implications are. (Don't forget to include the caretaker, who will need to be able to spend money on repairs, cleaning materials etc as well as monitor energy use.)
- Start the detailed planning for using standards grant money and resource spending.
- Calculate the amount available for Special Educational Needs and begin to take decisions for spending in September at the beginning of the new year. . . it is assumed that the summer term spending will already have been built in.

❏ April–July
- This is the time for consolidating the current spending that is related to the School Development Plan.
- Continue to check spending against all budget headings each month.
- Put children into classes for September and allocate teachers and teaching assistants that will be available.
- When classes are known, target special needs and begin recruiting SEN assistants/teachers etc.
- Monitor spending of standards fund grants.

❏ September–October
- Check costs of teachers and teaching assistants for mainstream classes.

- Check costs of SEN assistants and teachers.
- Make sure that large resource expenditure is in place for the beginning of the school year.
- Monitor current SDP and begin discussions for a new plan together with potential costs.
❏ November
- Repeat the cycle.

The sheer scale of the problems associated with the budget should be obvious. They are mainly linked to monitoring spending, the time taken to do this, the time that needs to be set aside for meetings with teachers and governors, how to allocate resources, and the kinds of decisions that need to be taken about staffing that may not always be to everyone's liking. What also needs to be made clear is the vital link between finance and teaching and learning. If the School Development Plan is thorough and the priorities are linked directly to the budget then it is more likely that standards will be raised. This can only happen, however, if, on the wider scale, the budget can provide for the appropriate number of teachers to make what happens in classrooms as effective as possible.

Dividing the budget

The budgeting process is driven by the School Development Plan which will help towards how the money that is available is divided. However, this is not a large amount once the cost of a teacher for each group of approximately 30 children and other salary costs have been taken out. Having said that, this is the amount that will determine whether you can allocate appropriate amounts to defined areas so that they make a difference in maintaining and improving the teaching and learning process.

Table 4.7 is not a definitive list but it is a way of developing basic budget headings. The estimated expenditure, while not being fixed, has eventually to have a fixed amount of money allocated to it, which should be close to either covering the costs in the case of energy or close to meeting the particular financial needs of an area such as furniture and caretaking materials.

Managing a budget does give schools an extra flexibility to manage their own priorities. Whether such independence and choice outweigh all the additional responsibilities is a matter for debate.

Monitoring the budget

The headteacher and the governors' finance committee need to work

Table 4.7 *Basic expenditure, estimated expenditure and unpredictable costs*

BASIC EXPENDITURE	ESTIMATED EXPENDITURE	UNPREDICTABLE COSTS
❏ Salary costs, including long-term sickness and any other insurance related to sickness	❏ Energy costs such as gas, electricity and fuel oil	❏ Unexpected repairs or health and safety issues
❏ Contents insurance Bought-in contracts for repairs to equipment, maintenance of IT	❏ Premises repairs and refurbishment {there is a large pool of money as capital funds for planned maintenance)	❏ Unforeseen curriculum needs, eg new central initiatives (there are usually extra funds provided)
❏ Bought-in services such as libraries and museums	❏ Materials	❏ Inaccurate costings of estimated expenditure, eg a larger energy bill, higher photocopier costs
❏ SEN costs for statemented children	– Furniture – Teaching consumables such as paper, pens, books, paints etc	
❏ Rates, ie buildings and water	– Teaching resources such as books, computers, software	❏ Staff changes resulting in a higher-paid teacher being appointed (this could, of course, work the other way and result in a saving on overall costs)
	– Copier costs and TV licences/rental	
	– Administrative costs including telephone	❏ Fewer children being admitted or several children leaving, resulting in less income and a smaller number on roll

together with any LEA officers who are allocated to the school to monitor regularly how the budget is being spent. This doesn't mean that other teachers with small budgets of their own aren't accountable, but that a small group of people have an accurate overview of the spending situation. In order to evaluate the budget effectively there has to be decision-making processes already in place. The budgeting process has already been discussed but it needs to be stressed that planning the budget carefully and thoroughly is essential. There are three stages of planning where the success is measurable and therefore more easily monitored. They include:

❑ An effective decision-making process which coordinates what the budget has to provide.
❑ Everyone needs to know what choices are available and what will happen if certain choices are accepted or rejected.
❑ There needs to be an annual cycle of review, planning and implementation which brings together all the relevant parts of the budgeting process.

Governors have to delegate day-to-day budgetary decisions to the headteacher and, after the initial setting up of the budget in March, either work with them, or keep a watching brief by receiving regular budget reports. Delegation, responsibility and accountability are at the centre of the school's responsibilities for controlling their own finance.

IMPORTANT POINTS

This chapter has suggested the importance of the school's management organisation and the crucial partnership between the school, the governors and parents:

❑ Each school needs to be aware of how its hierarchical structure and its place on the results–relationship continuum affects how effective it will be.
❑ There are close links between the internal organisation of the school and external influences. For example, class size, which is of enormous interest to parents, can be dependent on the number of teachers available and the number on roll as well as the amount of money that is available through the budget.
❑ Working with governors and providing them with all the information that they need to do their job is essential, especially in the key areas of the curriculum and the inspection process.
❑ Parents are also partners in the school and can improve the school's effectiveness if the school communicates with them, shares what it is trying to do and allows parents to be part of the process.
❑ The school budget is linked closely to the School Development Plan and can influence all areas of school organisation. It has to be planned carefully with governors and monitored closely.

5

THREE PROBLEM AREAS

The three problems that this chapter is concerned with are conflict, stress and how we manage time. They can all be destructive, reduce effectiveness and prevent standards being raised. Teachers often feel a sense of panic about the amount of work that has to be done and the lack of time in which to do it. There are also colleagues whose personalities and attitudes are such that they are difficult to work with and often difficult for headteachers to manage. If conflict remains unresolved it can create more stress and the school is in a spiral of debilitating problems which will not help when developing effective relationships or successful working teams.

MANAGING CONFLICT

Raising achievement will not happen at all unless all adults are able to work productively together to maintain and improve standards. Unfortunately, even in the most effective schools, there is conflict of some kind. It is inevitable because there are bound to be different personalities, points of view, ways of working and differences in terms of power and status.

But, as Everard and Morris (1985) in *Effective School Management* suggest: 'Conflict in the sense of an honest difference of opinion resulting from the availability of two or more courses of action is not only unavoidable, but also a valuable part of life. It helps ensure that different possibilities are properly considered. . .'.

Headteachers have to manage the differences that lead to conflict so that the people involved can develop and grow. It is also true to say that having to manage the kind of conflict that arises because of differences of educational opinion is better than being in a position where everything stays the same and stagnates because there is a lack of interest and an abdication of responsibility for new ideas and change.

Dealing with conflict

Conflict can lead to positive and useful problem solving and change. It can, as we have already recognised, be extremely destructive. This is why the management of conflict should be part of every school's ethos and culture. Developing and managing good working relationships needs time and effort but is essential if conflict is going to be reduced, and a cooperative and collaborative working atmosphere will enable headteachers and teachers to cope more readily with the stresses and strains of working in school. Everard and Morris continue the idea of collaboration and collegiality as ways to promote positive relationships when they suggest that preventing conflict can be achieved if all teachers have 'collective responsibility for the interests of the school' and if 'participative decision taking in which the views of interested parties are sought out before coming to a decision' is part of the school's ethos.

It is important to recognise that conflict is here to stay and that we must minimise the destructive forces of conflict at the same time as we minimise the stress that it causes.

The usual ways of managing conflict are by:

❑ *Ignoring it* – Unfortunately, ignoring conflict won't work and the disputes and factions it causes will not disappear. If it is ignored, it might seem to merge into the background but it is more likely that it will be suppressed and will reappear again when you are least expecting it.

❑ *Imposing a solution* – If a solution is imposed, it is more often done in an authoritarian way without considering the participants' concerns and feelings, and without really addressing the issue of why the conflict was there in the first place.

❑ *Facilitating a process where all those involved work out a solution* – This is by far the best way to resolve conflict but it is difficult and time-consuming. It does, however, offer a permanent solution, which involves negotiation, discussion, compromise and the ability of all participants to listen to each other.

Styles for handling conflict

Some people are better at resolving conflict than others and it is important to find out who they are and how they do it, because there are certain behaviour styles that do help to reduce conflict. Table 5.1 suggests five methods and it should be obvious that we are all capable of operating within

Table 5.1 *Conflict resolution styles*

1. Non-assertive style	This means that you prefer not to tackle the conflict and your behaviour is both unassertive and usually uncooperative. At worst, this style means that you will withdraw from any potentially threatening situations, but it is possible for you sometimes to wait for a better time and more appropriate opportunity to discuss the issue. If and when conflict does arise, some of your responses might include: 'I'd prefer not to discuss that now', 'Can't we talk about it later?' or 'That is really nothing to do with me'.
2. Agreeing style	This is still unassertive but usually reasonably cooperative. You will ignore your own needs and concerns to satisfy and meet the needs and concerns of your colleagues. You will probably spend a lot of time obeying when you would rather not, and giving in to your colleagues' points of view and demands. Some of your responses in a conflict situation might include: 'Yes, I totally agree with you', 'You've got a good point there and I agree with it' or 'Yes, you have certainly convinced me'.
3. Compromising style	This lies somewhere between being unassertive and being cooperative. You will work hard in finding ways to satisfy all parties who are in conflict with each other. It will possibly mean making concessions and meeting people halfway rather than insisting on all your own way. Some of your responses might include: 'I could agree with you there if you could accept that. . .', 'Let's see if we can agree on some things' or 'If we can agree on this, we will be able to find a quick solution'.
4. Competitive style	You will behave in an assertive but rather uncooperative way. You will use your own power and expertise to pursue your own concerns in any conflict situation. This will usually mean that you will either attempt to win,

Table 5.1 *(Contd)*

	defend your own particular position or stand up for your rights in a rather uncompromising way. Responses might include: 'Let me make my position quite clear', or 'Look, I know my way is the right one', 'If you don't agree with this, I will have to. . .'.
5. Problem-solving style	This is where you are both assertive and cooperative. You will aim to resolve the conflict by reaching a solution that satisfies both parties. To adopt this style you will need considerable interpersonal skills, honesty and a willingness to listen to different points of view. Responses might include: 'Look, it will be better if we work together on this', 'I feel this way about the problem. . . how do you feel?' or Let's work out how we can solve this'.

all five styles but that some are more useful in conflict resolution than others. There are more interesting ideas in Pedlar (1986) *A Manager's Guide to Self Development*, Rowland and Birkett (1992) *Personal Effectiveness for Teachers* and Smith (2000) *Raising Achievement in the Primary School*.

The non-assertive and the agreeing styles will be the least effective. They may help put any crisis off and lower the temperature of any disagreement but they will not resolve it. It is important to bear in mind the following points when using the styles of conflict resolution in Table 5.1:

❏ You need to work towards a win–win situation. This means working with colleagues, respecting any differences of opinion and being convinced that it is possible to find a mutually workable solution.
❏ Each person involved in any conflict should make sure that they take responsibility for their actions and behaviour and are prepared to face the consequences of their actions without blaming other people.
❏ Non-verbal communication is very important, eg eye contact. It is very important to look at colleagues as well as listen to what they are saying.
❏ Everyone involved in the conflict needs to know what it is about. All the details should be open to everyone and everyone needs to want to solve the problems that have led to the conflict.

❑ Separating the person from the deed is important. You have to work together so it is better to solve any conflict without long-lasting personal recriminations.

Criticism and conflict

Teaching is one of the few, perhaps the only, profession where public criticism from within the profession is the norm. Many teachers are made to feel vulnerable by this internal name-and-shame attitude and react badly and defensively to any kind of criticism, even if it is given in good faith to support professional development. In Chapter 3 it was suggested that it was possible to learn how to be assertive. Table 5.2 is similar in that it suggests a working script that will help you as a headteacher or senior manager to make critical, yet positive comments. It will not guarantee that the colleague who is being criticised won't react badly and create some kind of conflict, but it will give you a way into difficult situations which have to be confronted.

This is not the kind of name-and-shame criticism favoured by Ofsted's robust approach to monitoring what happens in schools through the inspection process. It seems to me that the only criticism that actually works and changes behaviour or actions takes place in a supportive no-blame culture.

There is further evidence for taking great care to avoid conflict through criticism in Handy's *Understanding Organisations* (1976). He suggests that criticism often arouses defence mechanisms and lowers self-esteem. He goes on to say that criticism is only helpful when it is given with a genuine liking for the other person and when it is related to specific instances.

While it should always be possible to relate criticism to a specific situation, it is not always possible for colleagues to like each other.

Reducing conflict by influencing colleagues

Certain kinds of behaviour can be provocative or can just create problems because of the kinds of attitudes that it presents. There are many ways of behaving that can create conflict and it will often depend on the circumstances. However, there are three specific ways colleagues behave that do make any kind of conflict resolution difficult:

❑ **Colleagues who grumble and complain** – They will do this frequently and about quite trivial things. Their negative attitude will dominate how they deal with work and their colleagues. It will seem to you that

Table 5.2 *A positive approach to criticism*

1. Describe the problem that is causing concern	It is important to choose an appropriate time and place that will help you make your first crucial points. For example: 'John, there seem to be some problems about you leaving early in the afternoon. You have left a few minutes after the children all last week and this week and missed an important staff meeting'.
2. Be more specific	Do this calmly, firmly and assertively, using 'I' as much as possible. For example: 'John, I've noticed that despite the policy for all teachers to remain in school for at least 20 minutes after school finishes, you usually leave much earlier'.
3. Insist on getting a reply	By doing this you are inviting a dialogue which should move towards some kind of agreement. For example: 'Is this what is happening?' or 'Is this the way you see it?' or 'Why do you think this is happening?' or 'Is this really happening on a regular basis?'.
4. Insist on change	Try to achieve this by agreement if possible. For example: 'How can we change this John?' or 'How can we improve this situation John?' or 'What do we need to do to make sure this doesn't continue happening?'.
5. Summarise the way forward	The intention is to briefly go over the points that have been raised and to suggest changes for the future. For example: 'So what we have agreed to do is. . .?' or 'So what you have agreed will happen is. . .?'.

their main aim will be to cast doubts on every new idea and to challenge anyone who expresses enthusiasm for anything. Unfortunately for the school, their grumbles and their negative attitudes can be contagious and can affect the morale of other teachers.

❑ **Colleagues who never contribute** – They will either say nothing or very little during meetings and their conversations in school will not add to the educational debate but will be largely about the weather or other inconsequential things.

❑ **Colleagues who are aggressive** – They can say hurtful things and be cuttingly sarcastic. They may also have an arrogant and know-it-all attitude and will try to dominate meetings and colleagues whom they see as vulnerable. They can put themselves across as self-appointed experts, but often don't know as much as they think they do.

Fortunately, such colleagues are not the norm and the majority of people who work in school do not instigate conflict to such an extent that steps have to be taken to resolve it.

Unfortunately, however, such colleagues do exist in small numbers and create a lot of problems.

On many occasions, however, conflict may be resolved by you, or any other colleague exerting the appropriate kind of influence on those involved in the conflict. Table 5.3 gives examples of six different ways of behaving that will help you do this. As you read each one, you might find it interesting to think how you can use this kind of behaviour and which of your colleagues might be influenced by you behaving in this way.

Table 5.3 *Ways of influencing colleagues*

Using your personality	You use your personality and charisma to suggest to colleagues that your power and influence are such that if your colleagues follow your example, they will have a much more exciting and pleasant future.
Using rewards	Any rewards that are offered, and there is a wide range that can be used, must encourage colleagues into a certain kind of behaviour. The reward must involve something that is actually worth having and will cause the person who is receiving it to offer something in return.
Influence through power and authority	Most people who work in school have some kind of legitimate influence, whether it is as a coordinator for a specific subject or because of some extra qualification that means they are an expert in some aspect of education. As head-teacher you will have a right to demand compliance from colleagues. This power, status and authority can be used to influence colleagues who do not have the same status and power.
Forcing colleagues to toe the line	This is about the ability to 'punish' those who don't comply with legitimate requests. This could range from not rewarding colleagues (even withdrawing praise can be useful) to

Table 5.3 *(Contd)*

	giving colleagues undesirable jobs to do. Such coercive tactics can isolate certain individuals, minimise their influence and reduce the number of opportunities to cause problems.
Being the expert	Using your influence in this way means demonstrating that you possess superior skills, abilities and knowledge. If you are able to do this and you also have power and authority, your colleagues are more likely to believe in you, which will make it easier for you to influence them.
Leading the group	Colleagues with whom you work closely, and this can be the whole school, will have their own attitudes, beliefs and ways of working that will have evolved over a period of time. Identifying with the group will give most colleagues a sense of personal satisfaction and a key factor will be that the 'leader' is respected to such an extent that colleagues will want to work productively with them.

Behaviour that can minimise conflict

It is only possible to influence colleagues through how you behave towards them. Obviously, arrogant, bullying and hostile behaviour will only serve to increase the tensions and conflict. By behaving in a positive way it is possible to reduce conflict so that the talents of both teachers and pupils can thrive. It is also about developing effective relationships. There are three basic skills that help you do this:

1. Make sure that you respect your colleagues. This will involve:
   - listening positively to them;
   - finding time to talk to them;
   - asking appropriate questions;
   - not patronising them.
2. Build up relationships that are based on genuine professionalism. This will involve:
   - responding naturally;
   - sharing feelings with colleagues;
   - being as spontaneous as possible;

- not being defensive;
- being yourself.
3. Empathise with your colleague's problems. (This doesn't necessarily mean agreeing with them or accepting them.) This will involve:
   - trying to understand the other person;
   - reflecting back the other person's feelings;
   - sharing similar experiences of your own.

An assertive way to solve conflict

Each person needs to realise, and this applies to teachers as well as headteachers, that everyone needs to work to reduce conflict and, at the same time, everyone has certain rights when it comes to working alongside colleagues in a stressful situation. Table 5.4 suggests some of the assertive ways by which conflict can be approached. It is important when looking at it to realise that everyone should be tied by the same set of constraints. In a school where this happens, there should be less conflict and fewer problems.

It is important to remember that different people do hold different points of view and that an honest difference of opinion resulting from the availability of two or more alternative courses of action is not only unavoidable but is often valuable.

Table 5.4 *Assertive ways to minimise conflict*

Everyone has the following rights:

❑ is able to say no at reasonable times without feeling threatened;
❑ has their own needs and is able to state what they are;
❑ is able to set their own priorities, which are not in conflict with those of the school or colleagues;
❑ is allowed to make mistakes without ridicule;
❑ is allowed to change their mind at appropriate times without causing problems to colleagues;
❑ is able to say that they don't understand;
❑ is allowed to ask for more time to complete a difficult task;
❑ can insist on deadlines being met and to meet deadlines themselves;
❑ expect praise and approval for successes;
❑ not to be responsible for every problem that colleagues have;
❑ is listened to and taken seriously;
❑ is given all the appropriate information and training for the job they have to do.

MANAGING STRESS

Stress in the workplace is a phenomenon of modern life, but it is especially acute in the 'caring' professions such as teaching. The numbers leaving teaching have increased dramatically during recent years and it is more difficult to recruit and retain good teachers, especially headteachers. Those remaining in the profession often have low morale and their level of job satisfaction is frequently low.

It is still a commonly held belief that stress in teachers is the result of personal and psychological factors that are more and more apparent because of the pressures of worsening discipline in classrooms, constant change and expectations that standards can continue to rise. It is important to recognise, however, that stress can be caused by the organisation we work in, how it is led and how it is managed.

Stress and the type of person you are

Elliott and Kemp (1983) take the view that the likelihood of succumbing to stress may be determined by the type of person you are. They describe two personality types:

1. **Type A people** – They tend to be aggressive, impatient, competitive and prone to heart disease. If it is suggested that they should relax more by taking up golf, for example, they are likely to take their aggression and impatience on to the golf course. They are likely to be highly stressed.
2. **Type B people** – They tend to be fond of leisure, not particularly hostile or competitive and are generally much more relaxed about life. They tend not to suffer from too much stress.

At the same time, however, there are certain characteristics of schools that can create stressful situations and stressful working conditions. When this is the case, the headteacher is responsible for monitoring the situation and managing it in such a way that the stress is reduced and no individual has severe and long-lasting problems that are associated with stress and the conditions that caused it in the first place.

Characteristics that lead to less stress

There has been a suggestion that high burn-out schools tend to have an autocratic management style, goals that only lead to academic achievement and clearly defined hierarchies, with individuals working alone rather than in teams. In low burn-out schools, educational objectives are flexible with less pressure for high standards and an organisational structure where teachers meet in both large and small groups to help take decisions and socialise. Table 5.5 summarises the characteristics within a school that seem to lead to less stress.

Table 5.5 *Characteristics that reduce stress*

Honesty	You need to know what you can do and then do it. If you say that you are going to do something then it has to happen. Also, if there are problems, it is important to make it clear to colleagues that these problems are happening. In other words, there is little subterfuge, very little window dressing and a lot of frank displays of hard work within the teams.
Approachability	Colleagues need to be able to approach colleagues with issues that need to be out in the open as well as with problems that need to be solved.
Openness	Good communication and open leadership, where decisions are shared and problems dealt with in a spirit of togetherness, are important.
Trust	There needs to be trust in the kind of teamwork that enables the school to run efficiently and effectively.
Values	An emphasis on tolerance and mutual cooperation will reduce stress because these values prioritise positive human relationships.
Sharing	Hierarchies breed dissatisfaction and the least stress occurs when there is a teacher culture of democratic participation. Teachers need to share values, knowledge, expertise, responsibilities and resources.
Responsibilities	Roles and responsibilities need to be interchangeable within a loose hierarchy where each teacher feels that they 'own' the decisions that have been made.
Knowledge and expertise	The school needs to be a learning community so that the considerable amount of knowledge and expertise can be shared, both formally and informally.

Table 5.5 *(Contd)*

Humour	Being able to share humour is important and the absence of humour suggests that there may be problems in working relationships.
Resources	All resources, including those that are human, need to be shared equally without favour.
Supporting	Collaborative support within groups of teachers helps each individual thrive emotionally, intellectually and spiritually. Teachers who are trusted and supported by their colleagues are willing to take risks to improve their teaching and raise standards.
Self	As well as understanding others, teachers need to understand themselves and their emotions and reactions to stressful situations.
Others	There needs to be a collaborative culture in schools where other people's strengths and weaknesses are understood so that their individual strengths are used to strengthen the work of the whole school team.
Understanding	Teachers need a high level of emotional understanding from each other and from leaders who know, understand and are interested in them as human beings.
Realism	The school needs to adopt a realistic approach to the work that has to take place. The kind of over-the-top conscientiousness that many teachers adopt can, in the long term, be counter-productive because it leads to tiredness and stress.

A more detailed analysis of these characteristics can be found in Troman and Woods (2001) *Primary Teachers' Stress*.

Identifying stress

Every headteacher must be able to recognise stress in colleagues and find ways of helping them reduce or get rid of the symptoms as well as the cause. Symptoms of stress include:

❑ tearfulness;
❑ frequent headaches;
❑ forgetfulness;

❏ high blood pressure;
❏ irritability;
❏ indecision;
❏ constant fatigue;
❏ waking in the small hours;
❏ insomnia;
❏ inability to relax;
❏ poor concentration;
❏ inability to complete simple tasks.

It is these kinds of symptoms that, if they persist, will affect how people work and how they relate to colleagues.

If you are aware of a colleague who is showing signs of stress, then you have to intervene and take preventive steps to minimise the stress. Figure 5.1 suggests at what stage you need to step in and take action. Intervening at the right time, or, if you are stressed, having someone intervene on your behalf can prevent stress escalating into a serious problem that can not only ruin individual lives, but damage the whole school.

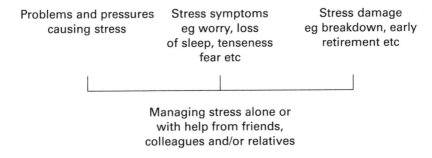

Figure 5.1 *Stress intervention points*

One way of identifying your stress, or that of a colleague, is to complete a personal stress inventory. Figure 5.2 has instructions and boxes to complete with your own responses. It can, of course, become part of your strategies for reducing stress and can be given to colleagues as part of their own stress prevention.

Causes of stress

There is no doubt that you can cause your own stress. If you are a Type A person, then you are more likely to be stressed than if you are Type B. There

1.	Write down what you think is causing your stress.
2.	Write down some of your physical and emotional reactions.
3.	Identify the build-up of symptoms and list them.
4.	List what you are going to do about the stress. (This might be your decision and yours alone, or the list may be arrived at because you have talked through the issues of stress with colleagues.)
5.	List some of the positive outcomes that should occur when you take some of the actions that you have identified.

Figure 5.2 *Personal stress inventory*

are other personal characteristics, including a fear of change, being an underachiever, having emotional problems at home etc. As a headteacher, it is important that you are able to recognise personal symptoms, but it is even more important that you are able to see how the environmental factors lead to stress. All the following areas are important and they can all cause problems related to stress:

❑ Relationships at work:
  – with superiors;
  – with subordinates;
  – with colleagues;
  – inability to delegate;
  – lack of team support;
❑ Organisational structure:
  – lack of participation;
  – no sense of belonging;
  – poor communication;
  – lack of any kind of power;
❑ Factors intrinsic to the job:
  – too much work and too little time to do it in;

- time pressure and deadlines;
- working conditions changing frequently;
❏ Role in the organisation:
  - conflict between several different roles;
  - too much responsibility for things;
  - too much responsibility for people;
  - too little responsibility;
  - too little management support;
  - under-promotion or over-promotion.

Ways to prevent stress

One way of trying to combat stress or prevent it happening in the first place is to use your own time in ways that helps you relax. It is important to take simple but important decisions like starting the day off properly with time to eat, changing your routines and, for example, going out for a mid-week meal etc. Table 5.6 is a list of activities and actions that should help prevent stress or alleviate some of the symptoms.

Stress can also be prevented by understanding certain fundamental factors related to the job that is being done and your capacity to do everything that the job requires of you. This will include the following:

❏ Know that you can't control everything.
❏ Know that there are some parts of the job that you can't understand.
❏ Don't expect to live up to everyone's expectations.
❏ Don't expect to be approved of by all your colleagues.
❏ Realise that running away from problems will not solve them.
❏ Don't expect to be right all the time.
❏ Know that you are capable of change, and that when you make mistakes you can handle them.

In Figure 5.1 there were stress intervention points where you could take certain actions to prevent the stress becoming debilitating. This is never an easy thing to do because different people react to a variety of approaches, and some colleagues, despite knowing what they should do, are often unable to act. When dealing with a colleague's stress, it may be necessary to distinguish between the different types of help that might be available and appropriate:

❏ **Changing the organisation** – This is making an effort to change the structure of the organisation if it is causing difficulties for colleagues.

Table 5.6 *Ways to combat stress*

❑ Make a good start to the day by relaxing over a healthy and unhurried breakfast.
❑ Avoid drinking too much coffee.
❑ Don't drink alcohol during the working part of your day.
❑ Don't try to do too much at once.
❑ Be better organised and prioritise.
❑ Don't try to be perfect: no one is.
❑ Rather than taking work home, why not come to work earlier or leave later, but not every day.
❑ Don't try to remember everything; use a diary of some kind.
❑ Try to avoid too many interruptions.
❑ Try to create a pleasant working atmosphere.
❑ If there are petty annoyances, try to speak out calmly and tactfully.
❑ Talk through any problems with colleagues.
❑ Take proper breaks, especially at lunchtime.
❑ Make sure that you are getting an appropriate amount of exercise and sleep.
❑ Make sure that you are eating properly and healthily.
❑ Make sure that work and relaxation are balanced.
❑ Say no in a constructive way.
❑ Consider trying to change your role in school.
❑ Consider changing jobs.
❑ Assume that there will always be some problems that are difficult to solve.

For example, schools often have entrenched routines and are organised in such a way that no one ever questions why certain things happen in certain ways. All kinds of things, including how breaks and lunchtimes are supervised, how pupils move around the school, which children are allocated to which teachers, may all be causing tension, conflict and stress. Some or all of these problems could be solved by making organisational changes.

❑ **Offering good advice** – This is really about giving your opinion based on your view of what has happened and what the situation is. For example, if a colleague is worried about how he or she is dealing with children with emotional and behaviour difficulties in his or her class, there should be systems where advice and help can be offered from you or from other colleagues.

❏ **Teaching colleagues** – This is about helping a colleague acquire the skills necessary to get out of a particular situation or solve a particular problem. It is closely connected to staff development and should be a key issue in school development and raising standards.

❏ **Providing colleagues with information** – Everyone needs the appropriate information that helps them do their job. For example, if a new teacher does not have the necessary information about the routines that have to be followed for serious cases of misbehaviour, then they may well feel inadequate if what they are doing doesn't work.

❏ **Taking action** – This is about actually doing something for a colleague, that is, taking direct action. If a colleague is really having difficulty setting achievable objectives in their short-term planning, then someone needs to sit with them and work through a few activities with them. This, of course, can be followed up with some staff development.

❏ **Counselling** – This is about exploring a problem with someone, looking at alternative ways of solving it and dealing with it so that they can begin to take decisions about solving the problem themselves. Counselling is not easy, but having a 'friend' to talk through problems and difficult situations can often lead to reduced stress.

Many of these techniques will involve making the right decision for a particular colleague at the right time. It is not possible to list the causes of stress and then match this against a technique that will help. Different people will need different kinds of support and headteachers and senior teachers need to be aware of this because, as we all know, stress can be destructive and can prevent achievement being raised because it stops those who are stressed from doing their jobs properly.

THE MANAGEMENT OF TIME

It is impossible to manage time. What we can do, however, is learn to manage ourselves and what we do each day in relation to time. Doing this effectively is very important because doing it badly can affect how stressed we are. Also, if there is a colleague who works with you who is constantly missing deadlines and rushing around panicking and interrupting other colleagues because of their poor time management, you have the potential for a considerable amount of conflict. So time management is important and yet at its simplest level, all it is about is planning your time effectively and recognising that as schools become more complex, the more important planning becomes a means of responding to and dealing with this increased level of complexity. All headteachers and, I would argue, everyone who works in school needs to be calm, well organised, thoughtful about educational issues, conscious of what is happening throughout the school, influential, and open to and aware of outside influences. At the same time everyone needs to be able to do the following:

❏ Plan what needs to be done and when it should be done.
❏ Control what we need to do to keep ourselves on target so that we can carry out the plans that have been made.
❏ Follow through what we start to the finish, rather than skip from one task to another. If we are interrupted, we should make sure that we have the time to go back to the task in hand, or at least leave it at a stage where we can easily pick up the threads again.

What is it possible to do?

You need to be able to make lists and then more lists and do most of your thinking about your use of time on paper because establishing priorities, things to do, and placing these in categories or levels of importance will be crucial to your success. First of all, you need to understand what you actually have to do and ask the questions: What is the situation now and what is my job about? This is an area of potential conflict because there are probably differences between where you are and where you would like to be, and what you want to do and what is being demanded of you. If you are serious about analysing your use of time, one way of doing it is to make a time log and write down what you do each hour of your working day. Alongside each entry, identify whether this was an imposed task, or one that you planned to do to move the school forward.

At the same time, it is important to identify some personal traits about the best use of your time. For example:

❏ At what time of the school day are you at your best for difficult and complex tasks?
❏ Which parts of your job are you really committed to?
❏ Which parts of your job are you the most enthusiastic about?
❏ What most concerns you about your use of time?
❏ What effect is your use of time having on your leisure activities, social life etc?

Taking action and prioritising

If you are serious about making changes to your day-to-day activities in relation to time, then you have to be prepared to take action and make changes. It is easy to be unnecessarily busy, and those colleagues who are always rushing around and racing against time are not always the most effective. It is important to establish priorities and then to take decisions about what to do, when to do it and how to finish it. You should be ruthless in prioritising. Get rid of all those tasks that are not crucial to your job so that you can concentrate on the jobs that matter.

One effective course of action is to keep up a running list of priorities that is constantly updated, usually on a daily basis. It works like this:

1. Beginning on a Friday, list your priorities for the following week under headings of:
    – *high priority* – these need to be completed quickly or urgently;
    – *medium priority* – these can wait for a while but are important;
    – *low priority* – these need to be done eventually and shouldn't always be left on low priority.
2. On Monday morning check the list, adjust it if necessary and take action.
3. On Monday afternoon, just before you leave school, write your list for Tuesday based on the same system. Some of the medium priorities will now be more urgent and also there will be new high-priority issues based on what has happened during the day. It will also be the case that some of the original high priorities will remain as such because you didn't manage to complete them.
4. Repeat this pattern at the end of each day ready for the next day, remembering that on Friday afternoon, all the tasks that you set as high priority on the previous Friday should be complete, together with most, if not all, of the medium-priority tasks. It will also be useful to look at the low-priority tasks that you set earlier in the week and ask yourself whether they should be higher priority or whether they should be left off the list altogether.

This may seem rather long-winded, but it takes a few minutes each day and could save hours of time. In one way, making lists establishes some kind of order in what can be a job that frequently makes unreasonable demands on the time that is available. If you don't plan and prioritise, you run the danger of finding that each day will be spent with too many unforeseen problems rather than organised opportunities.

Using up useful time

Trying to do too many things at once and not recognising what needs to be done, who needs to do it and when it needs to be done is largely down to poor planning, which can be part of failings in the whole school planning process as well as the weekly and daily prioritising described earlier. It is hardly ever the total amount of time spent on a project or task that is crucial but the amount of high-quality uninterrupted time that has been organised and planned. The effective use of quality time will mean using it sensibly. This does not mean working for hour after hour without a break. If this happens your energy will decrease, boredom sets in and the work will be completed in a much less effective way. We are told to strive for excellence and there is a continuous drive to raise standards. This is not the same as always striving for perfection, which should be regarded as a neurosis rather than an aim. During each day and through each week, you will have planned, prioritised and put the plans into action. There will be times, however, when other people start taking over your time and this is certainly a problem for headteachers. A simplistic answer is to suggest that you will have to say 'no' when demands are made on your time that you don't need and that you don't want. In fact everyone should have the right to say 'no' at reasonable times. If everyone accepts that, it will reduce the possibility of conflict and go some way towards minimising stress.

Avoiding time wasting

There are a few general rules that will help prevent other people wasting your time in such a way that it prevents you from effectively managing the time that is available and also that will prevent you from wasting your own time in a similar way. Table 5.7 suggests some useful strategies.

Table 5.7 *Strategies for avoiding time wasting*

Limit conversations	It may be possible to save time by limiting the number of minutes that you will talk to colleagues. This should become quite acceptable and there is no need to be rude or too blunt if everyone understands the need to be brief.
Terminate conversations at an appropriate time	Limiting conversations may be a slow process with some colleagues. It is possible to terminate conversations by saying, 'Look, I've got to go and deal with something else now'. It is often difficult

Table 5.7 *(Contd)*

	to hold professional conversations with colleagues in school outside the time for teaching and planned meetings. If this is the case it is important to arrange to talk to colleagues at a time when you know that both of you have space in your schedules.
Allocate time	When you are planning your week it is important to allocate time slots for specific tasks. For example, office paperwork such as reading letters; making telephone calls; walking round the school; discussing issues with the caretaker, cook, secretary. But don't allocate all your time. People aren't machines and part of your day should revolve around talking to colleagues, parents, children etc.
Don't allow unexpected visitors or telephone calls	Certain colleagues, children, parents and governors will need to talk to you urgently and it is important to operate a screening process that allows this to happen. Most of the time, however, this is not the case and they are merely operating within their own time plans. You need to make sure that talking at length to someone which is unplanned does not disrupt your own plans in a way that is negative and unproductive for you.
Are meetings necessary?	The answer, of course, is 'yes'. If you are trying to work in a collegial and effective way, there will be lots of meetings. Plan them, use a tight agenda, start them on time and finish them at a time you have planned, but not before you have reached decisions and know who is doing what and when. Don't let other people put meetings into your schedule that affect how you want to work.
Don't procrastinate	Don't put things off because they are difficult. One way of cutting down on procrastination is to start the next day by doing something unpleasant that you have been avoiding for a long time. Once you have done it, the rest of the day will be relatively easy.
Cut things out	Check everything that doesn't give you a feeling of accomplishment or help you work more effectively. If in doubt cut it out.

Delegating

All headteachers have to delegate and it is a technique that sounds so simple but always proves to be very difficult. It is probably a trait of all headteachers that they always want to be personally responsible for everything and often feel that by delegating, they will be losing opportunities to be in control and overloading other colleagues with more work than they can handle. To delegate successfully, there has to be a level of trust and it has to be recognised that other people are able to be effective and successful. Some useful things to remember when you delegate are:

❏ You are able to delegate the authority to do a job, but not the responsibility for it; that remains with you.
❏ It is important to delegate to colleagues' strengths, not to their weaknesses.
❏ Don't overload colleagues with delegated work.

Bell (1989), in *Management Skills in Primary Schools*, suggests the kinds of questions that need to be asked about what should and should not be delegated. He recognises that identifying tasks that you will be happy to delegate is the first step because it is counterproductive to be delegating something that you don't really feel happy in letting go. It will also mean that you will be spending a lot of time watching, monitoring and looking over the shoulder of the colleague to whom you have delegated the task. It is important to consider the following issues when identifying tasks to delegate:

❏ Which of my tasks can already be done by some or all members of staff?
❏ Which of my tasks make only a small contribution to the total success of the school?
❏ Which of my tasks takes up more time than I can afford?
❏ Which of my tasks are not strictly related to my key targets?
❏ Which of my tasks are really the day-to-day responsibilities of a colleague?
❏ Which of my tasks cause problems when I am away because no one else can carry them out effectively?
❏ Which of my tasks would help members of staff to develop if they were given the responsibility? (Bell, 1989: 164)

Effective delegation, of course, has to be planned if it is going to save time and the tasks that have to be completed have to be linked to performance management targets, the School Development Plan and completion dates. Delegation is not a haphazard process.

Basic criteria for effective time management

Table 5.8 is a final summary of the importance of time management and some of the ways that it can be managed effectively. In every school, there needs to be a commitment to maximising everyone's use of time.

Table 5.8 *Criteria for effective time management*

❏ Don't lose sight of long-term goals when you are prioritising.
❏ Set aside some time each day for setting priorities for the next day.
❏ Make lists in priority order.
❏ Don't feel stressed about completing every task on your high-priority list.
❏ If you don't complete everything, make sure that it is added to your next list.
❏ Write things down and don't just rely on your memory.
❏ Delegate as many tasks as possible to colleagues who are capable of completing them.
❏ Make sure that the delegated tasks are based on performance management targets and tasks in the School Development Plan.
❏ Set yourself and your colleagues realistic deadlines.
❏ Some of the time will be taken over by unexpected events and crises. Don't be too worried and readjust your priority planing as necessary.
❏ Keep asking yourself whether you are using your time effectively. If you aren't, make plans to do something about it.

IMPORTANT POINTS

Working with colleagues who are stressed, who find managing their time difficult and who are often in conflict with each other can and does disrupt the processes and organisational structures that make the school function effectively and that help colleagues work together in order to raise and maintain standards:

❏ Conflict within a school can be destructive unless it is part of the educational debate and is an exchange of different views that will move the school forwards.

❏ Headteachers cannot ignore conflict. It has to be managed and steps taken to prevent it happening and minimise its impact.

❏ The prevention of conflict often involves criticising a colleague and their behaviour. It is important that this is done positively.

❏ Stress does affect certain characters and personalities more than others but schools as organisations do cause stress and need to be structured and led in a way that reduces the possibility of stress.

❏ Headteachers need to be good at recognising stress and to know how and when to intervene if they find that a colleague is suffering from stress.

❏ The causes of stress need to be identified and the appropriate changes made.

❏ Time is a very valuable commodity and it is important to plan how to use it.

❏ It is important to prioritise and avoid time wasting and time wasters.

❏ Appropriate delegation is essential but it can be difficult.

6

LEADERSHIP

Let's begin this chapter by focusing on poor leadership in school. To do this we must go to Chris Woodhead who, as Her Majesty's Chief Inspector of Schools, made some important comments in his 1997 annual report. He concluded that the following were characteristics of poor headteachers and ineffective leaders in school:

- ❏ rarely seen in classrooms;
- ❏ does not monitor teaching enough to know staff's strengths and weaknesses;
- ❏ fails to bring about improvements in teaching;
- ❏ unable to delegate and spends far too much time on routine paperwork;
- ❏ fails to assess whether the school is getting good value for money;
- ❏ creates a lack of a sense of purpose through weak leadership;
- ❏ fails to give clear objectives and targets thereby causing staff to waste time and energy;
- ❏ adds to discipline problems by not laying down clear rules for pupils and to support staff when they try to discipline children.

There are many different ways of trying to analyse both what a leader does and what makes leadership effective. For example, at one level a leader is the person who can influence what happens in school, determine what needs to be done and what needs to be changed, organise how it is done and know when it has been successful. It is also true, however, that leadership is about the ability to make all the structures, decisions, changes and activities meaningful. This doesn't mean manipulating colleagues and changing their behaviour to fit a prearranged norm, but it does mean the ability to give colleagues a sense of understanding of what they are actually doing in the school. In many ways, both these examples of leadership relate to the school's needs and the ability to understand these needs as well as being able to adopt strategies, attitudes and behaviours that would meet them. They would, if they were skilful and effective leaders, be able to recognise the needs of the tasks to be undertaken and how to achieve these tasks; be aware of the needs of the staff team as a whole and how to build and maintain these teams; and be able to recognise the needs of the individual within the staff team and know how to develop each individual's potential.

If we are trying to clarify leadership in simple terms, it is also useful to summarise the kinds of character traits which characterise effective leaders. Table 6.1 will add to these and divide them into specific management areas, but they will include: a sense of responsibility, concern for completing tasks, energy, persistence, risk taking, originality, self-confidence, the capacity to handle stress, the capacity to influence and the capacity to coordinate the efforts of others.

WHAT IS LEADERSHIP?

By introducing the concepts of leadership 'traits' and their relationship to different organisational roles we are actually moving towards recognising what leadership might be in certain contexts. There are, of course, many elusive definitions and many of them are related to the kinds of influence, direction, support, discipline and care over people that a specific person has. It is also true to say that the words 'leadership' and 'management' are often used loosely and yet are very closely linked together. Leadership, for example, is about change and taking people forward in a particular way, while management is usually about the organisation of systems, structures and processes. The links between the two are seen more clearly if we recognise that yet another definition of effective leadership includes:

❑ good goal planning and goal setting;
❑ effective design and use of structures and systems;
❑ efficient use of resources; good person management;
❑ a concern for outcomes which is balanced by a care for colleagues who have to deliver the outcomes.

If leadership is judged more by results than intentions, then the emphasis is on how a leader behaves rather than their plans, structures and policies. This complex combination of tasks, attitudes and skills means that those who are headteachers and leaders, as well as those who want to be, need to understand what exactly is the task of leadership in school and how their own performance and competence can be enhanced to meet the challenges that leadership presents.

Table 6.1 *Leadership traits and areas of school organisation*

MANAGEMENT	INTERPERSONAL	PROFESSIONAL
❑ Provides clear direction	❑ Good communicator	❑ Principled
❑ Proactive	❑ Supportive, considerate and caring to colleagues	❑ Clear vision on the quality of teaching and learning
❑ Takes decisions		
❑ Highly visible to staff and pupils	❑ Encourages individuality but remains responsible	❑ Clear understanding of curriculum change
❑ Delegates effectively		
❑ Shares, involves and develops others, including governors and parents		❑ Promotes systems and structures which demon-strate the values and beliefs that underpin the school
	❑ Earns respect	
	❑ Promotes trust	
	❑ Motivator	
	❑ Cooperative	
❑ Strategic planner	❑ Consistent	❑ Promotes corporate understanding
❑ Opportunistic	❑ Organised	
❑ Change manager	❑ Clear thinker	❑ Defines roles clearly
❑ Grasps awkward nettles	❑ Enthusiastic	
	❑ Realistic	❑ Fosters high standards and expectation, supported by consistent and effective monitoring and evaluation
❑ Crisis manager	❑ Confident but willing to learn	
❑ Contingency planner		
	❑ Capacity for hard work	
	❑ Copes well with stress	
	❑ Well adjusted	❑ Commitment to accountability for improvement
	❑ Sense of humour	
	❑ Wide personal interests	
		❑ Professionally reflective
		❑ Gathers and uses research data
		❑ Recognises and acts upon own personal needs

WHO CAN BE A LEADER?

Bell (1989), in *Management Skills in Primary Schools*, suggested that: 'Opportunities for leadership may be presented to an individual by virtue of his or her position in the school, but holding a particular office provides no guarantee that leadership behaviour will be forthcoming from the incumbent although the expectation is that this will be the case'.

Leadership in schools today is exercised at many levels and headteachers need to recognise that the leadership skills they have need to be transferred to other teachers. Teachers are, for example, leaders in their own classrooms because teaching is about influencing, directing, setting goals and objectives, and using appropriate resources to achieve those goals. In the case of subject coordinators, leadership frequently has to be seen as the management of resources, information and the structures that underpin the organisation of the school. At the same time, however, coordinators as well as deputy heads have to have influence over colleagues so that they can begin to direct and influence them. It is here that there are more similarities with the role of the headteacher as leader because we are beginning to take forward fellow professionals in desired directions with the same sense of purpose as our own. It is, in fact, about influencing and directing colleagues in professionally desired directions and purposes. Once we start thinking of leadership in these terms, we will need colleagues who have a deep knowledge of the curriculum and of associated pedagogy and assessment as well as excellent skills of communication, motivation and persuasion. We are now beginning to think in terms of headteachers and it is important to look at the NPQH criteria and standards because they emphasise the following as the key outcomes of successful headship:

❑ creating a positive ethos in the school – a 'productive, disciplined learning environment';
❑ ensuring that all teachers perform to the best of their ability in pursuing higher standards;
❑ ensuring effective and efficient use of the whole resource base of the school, human, financial and physical;
❑ securing commitment of the wider community.

It is these kinds of goals that suggest that candidates for leadership need to be able to lead through their own vision of what an effective school should be.

WHAT DO LEADERS DO?

In very simple terms, what leaders do is develop this very clear vision of where they should be taking the school. To do this, headteachers need to be able to do the following:

- ❏ be aware of relevant national and local developments;
- ❏ network with other headteachers;
- ❏ promote the school amongst the community and the parents;
- ❏ develop an accurate evidence-based view of standards and performance within that subject in the school;
- ❏ develop and communicate realistic targets and attainment standards.

Headteachers who are successful in doing this will develop and lead a school culture that is less about orders, mandates and instructions and more about persuasion, motivation and delegation. Teachers need to respect their leaders and because of this, much good change in schools is managed by the careful persuasion of individuals and groups that particular policies or practices are desirable or feasible and will lead to genuine progress.

In many ways, this kind of leadership is based on the simple premise of 'being considerate'. This means that there is considerable understanding of the views and attitudes of colleagues.

Leaders provide structures

When we act as leaders in school we set up structures which are the basic organisational building blocks of the school. For example, there are time-tables, communication networks, classes and other teaching groups, curriculum working parties, Special Educational Needs registers etc. Timetables can set up structures concerning the use of space; communication networks relate to staff meetings, working parties and record keeping etc. Structures for staff and children mean the setting up of class groups, allocation of teachers to classes, use of support staff etc. All leaders in school and especially the headteacher will be involved in:

- ❏ providing structures;
- ❏ maintaining structures;
- ❏ redesigning structures;
- ❏ adapting structures.

LEADERS' ROLES

Leadership roles in any school can be divided into three main types:

❑ **Roles relating to other people** – This is where leaders have to be competent in several areas of human relations. They have to act as a kind of figurehead who speaks at functions such as PTA meetings, curriculum meetings with parents etc, while at the same time being able to supervise, select, train, appraise and motivate the staff in the school.

❑ **Roles relating to the passing on of information** – There are three processes involved when information is shared in school. They are:
  – The need to monitor, fact find and assess situations by collecting as much information as possible from individuals, teams of teachers and from documents and reports.
  – Information that is gathered has to be disseminated and communicated to whoever needs it. This can be achieved by written memos, reports and policy documents or in face to face meetings.
  – The school's views need to be communicated to parents, inspectors, governors and education officers.

❑ **Roles involving taking decisions** – No school, department, Key stage or curriculum working party will be able to function successfully without taking decisions. This has been discussed in earlier chapters and is not always an easy task because it involves consultation and consensus. Headteachers have to be proactive in recognising the kinds of decisions that need taking as well as having strategies that allow them to respond to incidents as they arise. Decisions which involve change are always more difficult because they affect people and often mean changes to budgeting as well as responding professionally to the needs of individuals as well as the needs of the school.

Functioning effectively as a leader within these roles is far from easy. It is made more difficult because the kinds of difficult and complex decisions that have to be taken will involve people. When this happens, there is an immediate issue surrounding different personalities, viewpoints and philosophical stances. Each headteacher, as leader, has to make sure that they are committed to making it clear what has to be done, what needs to be organised and how it will affect individuals. This will mean that they will adopt certain styles and ways of working that help them absorb conflicting views as well as bring together diverse beliefs.

LEADERSHIP STYLES AND ROLES

We have already considered in earlier chapters such opposites as 'autocratic' and 'democratic'; 'directive' and 'permissive'; and in many ways it is unhelpful to suggest that one style is good and the other bad. For example, an autocratic style of leadership will not be particularly effective in a move towards collegiality where sharing a vision is one of the central aims of how the school is managed. However, if decisions have to be made about health and safety legislation or simple administration processes then there is no reason why an instant autocratic decision shouldn't be taken.

What is important about the style is that it should be appropriate for what is happening and for the task or process that is taking place. There is a distinction to be made here between 'process' and 'content' because all styles of leadership have to take into account completing tasks as well as bearing in mind the relationships between colleagues who are involved in the tasks. Table 6.2 is a simple but useful summary of a continuum of leadership styles which in many ways is similar to the results–relationship continuum discussed in Chapter 4. It uses four levels of behaviour or styles of leadership.

Table 6.2 *Styles of leadership behaviour*

Telling	This is high on task/content and low on relationships/process
Selling	This is high on task/content and high on relationships/process
Participating	This is low on task/content and high on relationships/process
Delegating	This is low on task/content and low on relationships/process

Everard (1986), in *Developing Management in Schools*, draws comparisons with the roles and styles a leader in the commercial world would be expected to use. They include:

❑ cause events to happen and know what he or she wants to happen;
❑ exercise responsible stewardship over resources and turn them to purposeful account;
❑ promote effectiveness in work done and search for continual improvement;

❏ be accountable for the performance of the organisation he or she is managing.

These criteria are no different to those that apply to leadership in schools and seem to include the two kinds of roles necessary for a leader to be successful, that is, one that derives from the office held, ie a headteacher, and the other from personal abilities and experience. Everard's list also dovetails neatly into the suggestion that if a leader is to be successful he or she needs to be able to:

❏ forecast what needs doing;
❏ plan how to do it;
❏ organise what needs to be done from the plans;
❏ delegate tasks to appropriate colleagues;
❏ coordinate and control what happens.

LEADERSHIP, ORGANISATION AND PLANNING

It was emphasised in Chapter 1 that a positive ethos doesn't just happen and that the headteacher's leadership and vision have a large part to play in developing a culture of high-quality teaching and learning. It is also true to say that establishing such an ethos will mean that leadership needs to be shared in a structured way with other colleagues and with governors. This is in no way devaluing the role of the headteacher but is making it clear that many aspects of leadership are not just about a leader acting alone, but are the sum of all the people within the organisation. Table 6.3 suggests some leadership attributes that are linked to the school's development planning cycle. A more detailed version can be found in the DES publication: *Development Planning: a Practical Guide* (1991).

If a headteacher as a leader possesses some of the attributes in Table 6.3 as separate entities, their leadership is likely to be less effective than someone who possesses many of them. If each of them exists separately, they will fail to complement each other in ways that will help ensure success.

THE EFFECTIVE SCHOOL AND LEADERSHIP

It must be obvious that there are clear links between the effectiveness of a school and the quality of its leadership, but it is important to emphasise

Table 6.3 *Leadership attributes linked to planning*

The headteacher as leader:

❏ has a vision of the ethos and aims of the school;
❏ inspires commitment to this vision and can create plans that give direction and purpose to its work;
❏ coordinates the planning and work of the school by allocating roles and delegating responsibilities within structures that support sharing and collaboration;
❏ is actively and visibly involved in planning and implementing change;
❏ is also ready to delegate and value the contribution of colleagues;
❏ is a skilled communicator, keeping everyone informed about important decisions and events;
❏ has the capacity to stand back from daily life in order to challenge what is taken for granted, to anticipate problems and to spot opportunities;
❏ objectively appraises the school's strengths and weaknesses so as to build upon the best of current practice in remedying deficiencies;
❏ emphasises the quality of teaching and learning, lesson by lesson and day by day;
❏ has high expectations of all staff and pupils;
❏ recognises that support and encouragement are needed for everyone to plan in a constructive and high quality way.

this point again. There have been many key books written about school effectiveness, including Rutter *et al* (1979) *Fifteen Thousand Hours*; Mortimore *et al* (1988) *School Matters: The Junior Years*; HMI (1977) *Ten Good Schools* and many more recent Ofsted reports. What they all have in common is that successful schools have high-quality leaders and the most significant factor in the success of such schools has been the effectiveness of the headteacher. This does not mean, of course, that any headteacher can possibly create an effective school all on their own. Any that think they can, whether through charisma, autocracy or the pursuit of extreme power, are doomed to failure. All coordinators, senior teachers and deputy head-teachers must have leadership skills and school leadership must involve many individuals rather than one single figurehead. The HMI (1977) study, *Ten Good Schools*, cited four characteristics shared by their headteachers:

❏ They communicated specific educational aims to staff, pupils and parents.

❏ They displayed sympathetic understanding of staff and pupils and were accessible.
❏ They showed good humour, a sense of proportion and dedication to the task.
❏ They were conscious of the corruption of power and power sharing was a keynote of the schools.

LEADERSHIP AND CHANGE

Leaders have to manage change. This is true whether it has been initiated in school or imposed from outside. To be successful they will need to be able to:

❏ recognise what motivates teachers;
❏ harness this motivation to the whole school in a way that will make it easier to achieve objectives and reach targets;
❏ recognise school demands for change;
❏ recognise the wider demands for change, from the LEA, central government and the local community;
❏ analyse the complex structures and relationships that exist in schools;
❏ simplify and have the ability to process complex information and material;
❏ set appropriate targets and goals;
❏ manage conflict;
❏ consult appropriately to achieve as much consensus as is appropriate.

There is a certain amount of overlap between this list and others in this chapter and there may well be other attributes that will help headteachers to make changes smoothly and successfully. It is important, however, to be aware of what will help in strategies for change because it is often the head-teacher who initiates it and sees it through and this means that there is considerable pressure on one person to perform minor miracles on a regular basis. On the other hand, we have already recognised that leadership should also be part of the skills of all teachers. If this is the case then it is important for changes also to come from colleagues other than the headteacher.

The whole process of change should be 'owned' by all those involved. If this happens, it will mean that they will also have a vested interest in making the change successful. Table 6.4 identifies three roles that leaders need to adopt if they are going to be effective leaders of change and new developments. Rather than be good at one, they will be more effective if they combine attributes of all three.

Table 6.4 *Attributes necessary for the successful leadership of change*

Giving solutions	This will mean that you are looking for solutions and not saying that you have all the answers. You will be helping colleagues solve problems and start to find their own answers. If you are good at this, you will know when and how to offer suggestions.
Acting as a catalyst	This is all about making colleagues think about what needs to change and, rather than think negatively, to begin to think more creatively and in different ways about how to make the change more successful.
Being able to help in the process of change	This will mean showing colleagues how to recognise and define needs, how to diagnose problems and how to begin to collect together the necessary information and resources that will lead towards the correct solution and ultimately the appropriate change.

The process of leading change

It may seem an obvious thing to say, but leading change is all about solving problems. When this is happening it needs someone who is able first of all to recognise the problem, secondly to find out why it exists, and thirdly, what needs to happen to make the necessary changes that will solve it. Those who are leading any kind of change would do well to consider a very simple process which was first suggested by Kurt Lewin (1947) in *Human Relations*. It is based on the assumption that change involves balancing two sets of forces; one set which are likely to help and promote the change and the other set which are likely to inhibit it. Figure 6.1 illustrates this and can be used in the following way:

1. Consider a change that you will lead.
2. Write down a description of all those people, situations and circumstances that will either resist the change directly, or will create a situation that will make the change difficult (these are the restraining forces).
3. Write down all the people, reasons and circumstances that will help promote the change.

Effective leadership will develop strategies to decrease the restraining forces and increase the driving forces, but this is far from easy and needs complet-

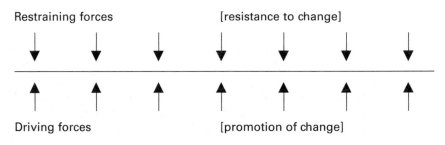

Figure 6.1 *Change force field*

ing in a structured and thoughtful way which involves colleagues and sees through the change to a successful conclusion. As leading change is such a vital part of effective school management, it will be useful to look at a structured way of doing it which builds on the three instructions for Figure 6.1 (the change force field) by including eight stages (Table 6.5).

In any school there will be colleagues who resist change for all kinds of reasons. They can be historical reasons in that they have always done things in a certain way or change can be threatening in that a teacher's professionalism often depends on doing things in a certain way. There are, however, different types of change and different ways of responding to it. It is useful to recognise the different types and to consider the different kinds of leadership that will make the change successful.

Leadership and employment change

This can be change because of new members of staff, retirement, redeployment or a reduction in the number of teachers that the school can afford. It is also about change affecting status. It can involve promotions, for example, which may leave other colleagues who have not been promoted feeling undervalued. In all these situations it is possible for confidence and competence to sag and both individuals and teams will be less effective.

Leadership and behavioural change

This is really about changes in attitude which can arise because of other changes or might, in fact, be desirable because a change involves a different way of working. This kind of change is mainly centred around those more 'sensitive' areas of the curriculum such as equal opportunities, gender, race

Table 6.5 *The process of leading change*

Stage 1	Identify and describe in writing the problem or the change that is needed. It is important to write it down and not just think about it.
Stage 2	Split the problem or change into the current situation and the desired situation. This will mean that, as leader, you have a clear vision of where you want to be.
Stage 3	List the driving and restraining forces. Don't be vague; be specific about such things as people, money, resources such as space etc.
Stage 4	Find a way to highlight the forces, restraining and driving, that are the most important.
Stage 5	Look at the restraining forces that you have highlighted. Write them as a separate list and alongside each one, list all the actions that could reduce or eliminate them.
Stage 6	For all the driving forces that have been highlighted, list the actions that could increase their power to help make the change process easier.
Stage 7	Work out from the responses to Stages 5 and 6 the most logical steps to take and in which order.
Stage 8	Check the logical steps and make sure that they are in order of priority. Use this as a final chance to change any and get rid of those that won't help you lead the change. It is also useful at this stage to suggest when the change will be completed. These dates may well be in the School Development Plan.

or Special Educational Needs. These are areas where change often implies a change in how colleagues might feel and it is more about personality and self than other, more neutral areas of the curriculum.

Leadership and procedural change

This can disrupt ways of working and can include such areas as timetabling, use of specific spaces in the school, changes to electronic registration, changes to the time of the school day, changes to ordering and distributing resources etc. Whatever it is, some colleagues will try to avoid it and pretend it isn't happening; some may even try to revert back to what they still perceive as the status quo. In some ways, these blocking tactics are understandable; after all, if we are honest, most of us prefer the safety of life as we know it, rather than the unknown of the consequences of change.

Leadership and organisational change

This is the broad swathe of change that is associated with how the school is organised.

It could be new Key Stage teams, different planning teams, an increased or reduced number of classes, or a change in which teachers are working with which class. There will be concern among all those involved in the change and this concern may manifest itself in denying what is happening and a lack of commitment. Some colleagues may feel stressed until they are reassured about and believe in the outcomes of the change.

Leadership and motivation

When a headteacher is managing change, their leadership qualities will be mainly to do with motivation. Successful motivation and, by implication, effective leadership requires much more than planning and action. It needs a knowledge of and an allowance for the way colleagues might feel. This is very important because it is the attitudes of teachers to leadership and change that can make or break any new initiatives, and it is the quality of the interpersonal relationships that will play a large part in determining how well the leader is able to motivate his or her colleagues. Day *et al* (1990) in *Managing Primary Schools in the 1990s* quote a survey that was conducted with 60 headteachers into school leadership. The criteria most commonly quoted could all fall into the category of 'motivational'. They included:

❑ sympathy towards the ideas of others;
❑ appreciation of others' points of view;
❑ understanding of and concern for others;
❑ compassion;
❑ approachability by staff, parents and children;
❑ the ability to deal with problems as they arise and 'still have a smile';
❑ the ability to inspire trust and confidence;
❑ tolerance, especially of opposing ideas;
❑ tact;
❑ willingness to praise and to be seen to praise;
❑ humour;
❑ the quality of being a good listener;
❑ the ability to cope with opposition and unpopularity as well as with support and encouragement;
❑ the ability to know when to pressurise and when to stand back;
❑ the capacity to be fair and just and to be seen as fair and just;

❏ the ability to lead, to guide, to cajole when necessary, to be loyal and supportive of the staff and to maintain enthusiasm despite any problems (1990: 20).

Many of the headteacher's leadership skills will need to be used with teams or working groups of teachers. What kind of leadership style or role to adopt will, to a large extent, depend on the stage of development of the team or working group. This will mean being able to:

❏ identify the team's stage of development;
❏ be aware of the range of approaches available;
❏ select the appropriate approach;
❏ possess and be able to use the ability to put whatever approach is effective into action;
❏ monitor the effectiveness of the approach and modify and make changes where and when necessary.

Motivating colleagues will occur most successfully when everyone has agreed on a particular course of action. The headteacher will then be able to lead by using a variety of skills which are largely to do with motivating the team through discussion so that a successful conclusion can be reached. Some of these skills will include:

❏ negotiating skills;
❏ summarising skills which form links between different ideas;
❏ questioning skills which open up the discussion;
❏ selecting the key points in an argument;
❏ clarifying discussion points;
❏ synthesising and evaluating different points of view;
❏ listening in order to respond to what is being said, including the hidden agenda of different members of the team;
❏ non-verbal skills which help identify people's attitudes and feelings through observing posture, gesture, facial expression etc.

NEGATIVE RESPONSES TO LEADERSHIP AND CHANGE

Most colleagues are able to work together to raise standards and most headteachers are able to lead, develop and motivate most colleagues. It would be naive to suggest, however, that all colleagues are reasonable.

When change has to be managed there can be many pockets of resistance. This resistance can be lowered if those who are leading the change are able to explain why the change is necessary and what the advantages are likely to be. Hand (1981) suggested that there were four categories of teachers:

❏ those who were frustrated in their ambitions;
❏ those who were happy to be in their final career posts;
❏ those likely to gain further promotion;
❏ those who were happy to be in their current post but who found it difficult to cope with the stresses caused by externally imposed innovation.

If we accept that all four categories can exist in every school, then it becomes obvious that if leaders, especially the headteacher, are trying to match individual and institutional needs during any process of change, there may be conflict created by the tensions between the two. If this is the case then it becomes even more important for leaders to take every opportunity to involve all the teachers from all four of the above categories. By doing this, everyone should be able to feel that they have some vested interest in the change and mistrust, rumour and misunderstanding will have been avoided. An effective leader will know that sharing information and allowing opportunities for discussion and, where necessary, complaint, will mean that any changes are more likely to be successful.

OFSTED AND LEADERSHIP

I want to end this chapter on leadership by going back to Ofsted. *Inspecting Schools: Handbook for Inspecting Primary and Nursery Schools* (1999) has a short section on leadership (pp 92–106). First of all, they categorise it into whether it is 'very good or excellent' or 'satisfactory or better' or the doom and gloom scenario of 'unlikely to be satisfactory'. Table 6.6 summarises the criteria for each category.

Schools need the sense of direction provided by strong leadership and leaders need beliefs and values that can shape the culture and values of the school and develop high-quality teaching and learning. Being decisive, forceful and, at the same time, consultative is one way of leading from the front and being recognised as a leader. Most leaders, however, have qualities that go beyond taking decisions and being forceful. Effective leadership is about being able to motivate colleagues. They have to be able to express enthusiasm and encourage professional growth and expertise. They should also be able to support colleagues and make them feel secure and positive

Table 6.6 *Categories for the quality of leadership*

LEADERSHIP THAT IS VERY GOOD TO EXCELLENT	LEADERSHIP THAT IS SATISFACTORY OR BETTER	LEADERSHIP THAT IS UNLIKELY TO BE SATISFACTORY
❑ All leaders in the school share a common purpose	❑ The leadership and management are clear about the school's strengths and weaknesses	❑ There is a significant amount of unsatisfactory teaching
❑ Children and their achievements are put first	❑ Some ways of securing improvement have been established	❑ There is a significant complacency amongst staff
❑ There are cooperative and coordinated teams	❑ Teamwork is well established	❑ Standards in school are significantly lower than they should be
❑ Assessment evidence is used well to set challenging targets	❑ The school has identified the right tasks for the future	
❑ Teachers reflect critically on how to improve learning and develop more effective ways of working	❑ Most staff share a common purpose and have taken steps to make their work more effective	❑ The headteacher and governors do not know the strengths and weaknesses of the school and are, therefore, largely ineffective
❑ The quality of teaching is monitored	❑ Staff with specific responsibilities are clear about what they are and how success will be measured	
❑ Coordinators have delegated responsibilities		
❑ There is effective follow-up to ensure tasks are completed	❑ Governors have a sound sense of the strengths and weaknesses of the school	
❑ Governors monitor performance		
❑ Governors have a good understanding of the strengths and weaknesses of the school	❑ Governors are working with staff in their efforts to improve	
❑ The governors and the headteacher		

Table 6.6 *(Contd)*

---

set the right
priorities for
development and
improvement
❏   The governors
help provide a
sense of direction
for the school

---

about change. All effective leaders need to be able to consult, work towards a negotiated solution and involve colleagues who will, because they have been part of the decision-making process, feel that they have a sense of ownership of how the school functions.

IMPORTANT POINTS

Leadership is a very complex issue and because of this there will be a considerable amount of overlap of the skills that are needed for a leader to work effectively within all their expected roles:

❏   Leadership is about motivating colleagues and taking them forward within a central core vision that is shared with them.
❏   Headteachers and to a considerable extent all teachers who are coordinators need leadership skills.
❏   They will create management structures within which clear and worthwhile decisions can be made.
❏   Certain leadership styles are appropriate in different circumstances but whatever style is used has to cause events to happen.
❏   The key to an effective school is an effective headteacher who will be capable of managing change successfully.
❏   Every school needs to take note of Ofsted's views on effective leadership.

7

MANAGING SUCCESSFUL TEACHERS AND EFFECTIVE TEACHING

In Chapter 6, leadership was discussed in relation to the expectations that Ofsted have when inspecting schools. *Inspecting Schools: Handbook for Inspecting Primary and Nursery Schools* (1999) makes it clear that: 'the leadership and management are unlikely to be satisfactory if. . . there is a significant amount of unsatisfactory teaching' (1999: 94). This means that what happens in every classroom needs to be of the highest quality and it puts effective teaching and learning at the forefront of every headteacher's key objectives. Chapter 9 will examine some of Ofsted's criteria for successful teaching and there will, inevitably, be some overlap because this chapter is going to look at various ways of understanding what effective teaching is, how to promote it and how to monitor whether it is happening in every classroom. What is good teaching and how it is recognised will also be dependent on both the ethos of the school and the teaching and learning policy which was discussed at some length in Chapter 2. There are many lists of criteria for 'good' teaching and here are three of the most basic ways of looking at effective teaching characteristics. One of the simplest starting points is the six key skill areas which should be taught because they not only help learners improve their present learning but will enhance their future performance in education, work and life. These skills must exist in all primary schools because they are embedded in the National Curriculum and are described in detail in *The National Curriculum Handbook* (DfEE 1999). They include:

- ❑ communication;
- ❑ application of number;
- ❑ information technology;
- ❑ working with others;
- ❑ improving own learning and performance;
- ❑ problem solving.

Secondly, teachers need to be able to demonstrate that they are effective professionals who challenge and support all children to do their best by:

❑ inspiring trust and confidence;
❑ building team commitment;
❑ engaging and motivating children;
❑ analytical thinking;
❑ taking positive action to improve the quality of children's learning.

The third and final shortlist also suggests that effective teachers exhibit the following characteristics:

❑ They ask why.
❑ They are conceptual thinkers.
❑ They have the ability to see patterns.
❑ They use data and the evaluation of results to plan lessons thoroughly.
❑ They are able to analyse more and more complex situations.

ASSERTIVE TEACHING

Managing and controlling what happens in the classroom is a key issue for teachers and has to be the most important aspect of a headteacher's managerial role. At the same time, much of the professional development of teachers has to centre around the kind of targets that are set during performance management and the tasks defined by the School Development Plan. One of the most important aspects of both these tools for school improvement will be how to maintain and raise standards, and at the centre of this will be improving teaching and learning.

Teachers are not infallible. They are hard-working, have the usual human frailties, suffer moments of impatience and irritability and occasionally make the wrong decision and take the wrong course of action. Most teachers, however, have a fund of skills, expertise and knowledge which they can draw on to develop and maintain classrooms where teaching and learning take place positively and effectively within an atmosphere of firmness, fairness and consistency. It has been a commonly held view both by teachers themselves and certainly by many headteachers that the group management skills that are necessary in the classroom are natural gifts that you either do or do not possess. It may be true that some teachers, and I am convinced that this is a small minority, are naturally blessed with such talent. However, it is damaging to many teachers, who may be experiencing crises of confidence, to lay the blame on their own inadequacies rather than on their lack of particular skills, many of which can be learnt and can be part of a programme of professional development.

Perhaps the biggest problem that teachers have had to face over the past few years has been the constant erosion of their authority and society's assumption that much of what is wrong with Britain today can be blamed on teachers and schools. As well as lowering the confidence of all those who work in schools, this attitude, which is nurtured in the press, must take much of the blame in making the recruitment and retention of young teachers difficult. A further problem is pupils who challenge authority and behave inappropriately and badly. Such children can sap energy, create rifts between teachers and children, and develop a tense and negative atmosphere.

As headteacher, it is important to make sure that your school has classrooms which are positive, creative and very much work orientated. This will mean that each teacher is able to be 'assertive' rather than 'passive' or 'aggressive'. Figure 7.1 suggests a very quick activity for teachers to use to find out whether they are able to recognise what 'assertive' actually means. If the responses are discussed it can also be used to recognise the kinds of attitudes and behaviour to avoid in the classroom.

If you are using Figure 7.1 as an activity with teachers, they should have placed AS alongside the following words: *confident, in control, firm, fair, thoughtful* and *knowledgeable*. A further 10 minutes could be usefully spent thinking about how behaving in these ways will improve colleagues' teaching styles, classroom management skills and general all-round teaching ability. It will also be important to stress that teaching in your school will be much more consistent and effective if all teachers are able to avoid aggression by not getting *angry, volatile, hot-tempered* or *out of control*. If they do behave in these ways their teaching is more likely to be inappropriate and it could well be counterproductive in their attempts to raise standards. Equally, passivity and the kinds of behaviour associated with it, which include being *put upon, lacking in confidence, timid, mild, meek* and *complacent*, is more likely to lead to the kinds of discipline and classroom management problems that also inhibit high-quality teaching. Before looking more closely at what assertive teaching is and why it is an appropriate style, let's summarise ways of defining 'aggressiveness', 'assertiveness' and 'passivity':

❏ **Aggressiveness** – This is to be avoided because it means getting your own way by making children feel useless, worthless or small. It usually involves conflict by causing hostility and a sense of unfairness.

Read each word and alongside each one write AS if you think behaving in this way is Assertive, AG if you feel it is Aggressive and PA if you think the word suggests Passivity.

angry	volatile	confident
put upon	in control	lacking in confidence
hot-tempered	dominant	timid
firm fair	thoughtful	
knowledgeable	mild	violent
out of control	meek	complacent

Figure 7.1 *Behaviour and attitudes in the classroom*

❑ **Assertiveness** – This is about being responsible for your own behaviour by respecting the children in your class. An assertive teacher is able to say what they want and feel but not at the expense of the feelings of the children. It is also about being self-confident and positive in the classroom and having the ability to influence classroom relationships either so that conflict doesn't arise in the first place or by reaching acceptable compromises.

❑ **Passivity** – This means ignoring your own interests and allowing the children in your class to manipulate each other and you. It often means denying your own feelings by not being active and proactive and not recognising that you are the professional with needs and goals.

So to be assertive, your teachers need to be able to behave in the following ways:

❑ Have respect for themselves and the children.
❑ Understand children's points of view.
❑ Show self-confidence and a positive attitude.
❑ Do not expect to win in every situation.
❑ Do not expect always to get their own way.
❑ Avoid confrontation in the classroom, but when it happens, handle it in such a way that there is an acceptable compromise.

PROFESSIONAL EFFECTIVENESS

If all the teachers working in your school are assertive, they will be more likely to be successful classroom practitioners who are able to use a wide variety of successful teaching and classroom management skills. Even if this is the case, however, it is still important that they are competent in the following six areas, which all relate to their 'professional effectiveness'. If they are not, of course, it is the responsibility of the headteacher and other appropriate team leaders to make sure, through performance management targets, that development and training opportunities are available.

1. Curriculum knowledge

They should have a thorough and up-to-date knowledge of the teaching of their subjects and take account of wider curriculum developments which are relevant to their work. This will mean that they will:

❏ be able to use sound teaching techniques relevant to the subjects they are teaching;
❏ know their subjects in sufficient depth to be able to teach effectively;
❏ be aware of and take account of all the relevant primary curriculum developments even though some of them, eg the foundation curriculum, might not necessarily be thought to be immediately relevant;
❏ be aware of all the national strategies that are relevant to primary schools.

2. Lesson planning

Successful lesson planning will rely on a thorough knowledge of both the subject and the class of children that is being taught. It will involve teachers:

❏ using their knowledge of individual children's learning needs to plan individual lessons and sequences of lessons;
❏ targeting individuals and groups effectively;
❏ setting clear lesson objectives;
❏ communicating objectives to children;
❏ using homework effectively;
❏ using other opportunities for promoting learning outside the classroom.

3. Using appropriate teaching and learning strategies

This will involve being able to use a variety of teaching styles which not only suit the subject of the lesson but also the range of abilities, age of the children and the children's attitudes to learning. It will involve:

❏ using the appropriate teaching strategies to motivate all the different groups of children in the class;
❏ understanding the special educational needs of individual children and being able to target appropriate teaching and support;
❏ choosing the right strategies to maintain high levels of behaviour;
❏ adopting a range of techniques to deal promptly and effectively with misbehaviour;
❏ managing the teaching time effectively to provide a broad and balanced curriculum;
❏ making sure that there is a full range of appropriate resources available for all children;
❏ using all the available teacher and teaching assistant support effectively.

4. Using assessments to plan teaching objectives

This will mean encouraging all teachers to use all the appropriate assessment evidence which in most, if not all, schools will include: end of Key Stage national tests, QCA tests at Years 3–5, NFER English tests and any other internal assessments such as reading ages. Using these assessments will need to involve:

❏ evaluating children's progress against similar schools using national and local data;
❏ using the assessments to set realistic and yet challenging targets for improvement;
❏ using assessment as part of everyday teaching to monitor children's progress;
❏ using assessment to adapt teaching approaches as and when necessary;
❏ providing appropriate support by regularly referring to assessment and pupil progress;
❏ reporting children with specific needs to SENCo as required.

5. The quality of the teaching ensures pupil progress

This aspect of successful teaching has direct links with assessment because children's progress can only be measured by assessing them in some way. At the same time, however, and this is a direct link to other aspects, progress will be greater if appropriate teaching styles are used.

It is one of the functions of effective teaching that children do make progress and it is one of the headteacher's duties to see that teachers work in ways that ensure that progress is made. Teachers need to do the following to show that this has happened:

❑ Match children's prior attainment against present attainment.
❑ Measure the progress of their children against external data such as national test scores.
❑ Measure children's progress against other school data.
❑ Use any value-added data that the school is involved in, such as the progress shown from baseline to Year 2 and from Year 2 to Year 6.
❑ IEPs should be used to monitor the progress of children who are on the school's SEN register.

All children are capable of making progress, and raising achievement should be the norm. Headteachers have the responsibility of making sure that this is part of the school's ethos. To do this they need to be able to make a professional judgement about each teacher's ability and to use professional development and training opportunities when and wherever necessary. The most appropriate approach is for headteachers to do the following:

❑ Monitor each class for consistent progress for the majority of children when compared to prior attainment.
❑ Be aware of the peculiarities and problems presented by different classes, eg a high incidence of SEN children, more statements than usual, problems associated with E2L etc.
❑ Is progress made across the range of children in each class, ie children of different behaviour, background and/or ability?
❑ It is also important to monitor whether the children's progress compares favourably, or otherwise, with internal data for previous years and with local and national performance data.

6. Professional attitudes and characteristics

This is a very wide-ranging quality and some aspects of it will be followed up later in the chapter. It is about the kinds of characteristics that effective teachers are able to demonstrate on a daily basis and which will govern how successful they are in meeting the challenges of the five previous characteristics. There are five subsections, which include:

A   Teachers who inspire confidence and trust
- They are committed to the development of their children.
- They respect the children in their class.
- They are able to influence their children through their integrity and professional confidence.

B   Building working teams of children
- Recognising and rewarding achievement.
- Having the skills to tackle issues which might hinder a child's progress.
- Being able to set up groups of children who are able to work together constructively.

C   Motivating children
- Agreeing clear expectations with children.
- Motivating children for whom learning is not always easy.
- Making learning relevant and interesting.
- Targeting specific children for extra support and encouragement.

D   The ability to think clearly
- Identifying cause and effect in pupils' learning.
- Using knowledge of the 'whole' child to get them to do their best.
- Comparing past teaching strategies and successes with ones that are currently in use and making links to gauge the best learning strategies.

E   Improving the quality of children's learning
- Gathering all the information that is available to guarantee improvement.
- Anticipating difficulties and planning ahead to reduce their impact.
- Resolving problems before they become too far advanced.

The Teacher Training Agency, *National Standards for Qualified Teacher Status* (1998) and *Threshold Assessment: Guidance on Completing the Application Form* (2000), suggest a wide range of detailed criteria for making judgements about successful and effective teaching.

EFFECTIVE TEACHER BEHAVIOUR

At the beginning of this chapter, three essential ways that teachers must behave were mentioned briefly. They were 'firm', 'fair' and 'consistent'. Behaving in these ways is the umbrella under which effective teaching takes place. If there is to be a consistency of approach in each school, it is also important to develop the attitude among teachers of using four more teaching and classroom strategies. They are:

❑ **Praise** – This means that every classroom, as well as the ethos and culture of the school will involve far more praise than criticism. There will be quiet praise which is part of routine classroom activities, sharing praise among classes and year groups, and the kind of public praise that takes place in assemblies.
❑ **Care** – All teachers need to show their children that they care, both about their work and the attainment of high standards and about their lives both inside and outside the school.
❑ **Flexibility** – There will be times when teachers find that teaching in a certain way just does not work. It is important that the school's attempts to standardise teaching methods and achieve a sense of a consistent approach to teaching does not remove creativity and that there is room for more flexible approaches if it is found that one teaching method is not working.
❑ **Perseverance** – This is really that old cliché: if at first you don't succeed, try, try again. Headteachers must make sure that, despite the need for a consistent approach, there is room for changes in style and for the 'flexibility' that is needed for change, because perseverance can mean carrying on in a particular way to achieve success, but it can also mean trying something different to achieve the same ends.

Table 7.1 lists a range of teaching styles which are related to the six areas in the previous section and to the umbrella concepts of *flexibility, fairness, consistency, firmness, perseverance, care* and *praise*, but which also provide a slightly different emphasis and if used well can make teaching within the previous categories even more effective. For headteachers the list could provide another useful checklist when monitoring the consistency of teaching quality within the school.

Table 7.1 *Teaching styles*

❑ Lessons are planned so that the work that is set extends and motivates all children.

❑ Teachers arrive in the classroom well before the children.

❑ Praise is emphasised more than criticism, but teachers are critical of both behaviour and work when it is appropriate.

❑ Pupils are included as far as it is possible in planning their learning.

❑ The level of attainment that each child brings to specific tasks is taken into account when setting targets for individual children.

❑ Children are encouraged to work cooperatively.

❑ Realistic goals and deadlines are set.

❑ Positive on-task behaviour is the norm.

❑ Discipline and control are quiet, firm and help the teaching and learning process.

❑ Skilful questioning encourages children to think and use the knowledge that they already have.

❑ Punishments are fitted to the 'crime' and the individual. There are no blanket punishments against the whole class.

❑ Humour, laughter and smiles are used to create a positive atmosphere for teaching and learning to take place.

❑ There is constant and positive teacher interaction with children as they work on tasks.

❑ Good work by individuals is used to stimulate other children.

❑ Continuous feedback is provided so that children are aware of the quality of their work, their efforts and their behaviour.

Styles for reducing disruption

If we do accept that part of assertive teaching is about being firm, fair and consistent, we should also recognise that it is about teachers having the techniques to state clearly to children what is and is not acceptable behaviour. The techniques used by teachers should be broadly consistent and should be monitored for their success by headteachers on a regular basis. There are many books on behaviour management and this is not one of them, but there are some simple techniques that are worth promoting in primary schools. They are all based on the premise that teachers should say yes as often as possible but when they say no, they really mean it. In other words, every child should know what will happen, ie the consequences if they behave in certain unacceptable ways. One of the advantages of this method is that it is relatively quiet and unobtrusive and most teachers are able to use it and carry on teaching with minimal disruption to their lesson:

1. Three lives – There are several variations and it is probably quite a well known technique.
    ❏ The teacher specifies what behaviour is inappropriate and what the consequences will be if anyone behaves in that way, eg don't call out to answer questions, don't run in the corridor etc or you will miss a play time, have time out of the classroom etc. If a child does behave in this way, write their name on the board with a cross against it and tell them that they have used up one of their three lives. Repeat this if necessary with other children and with further crosses. A variation is to allow them, by behaving in a correct and appropriate way, to buy back lives. Once they have three crosses, what the teacher specified as a consequence must take place.
    ❏ There is a second similar method which puts the ownership of the act of losing lives on the child. Specify the inappropriate behaviour and the consequences for behaving in that way and make it very clear that you are giving the child three lives. They have the lives and if they behave in the specified inappropriate way then they are giving them away. It is they who are choosing to lose them. With this method, the teacher cannot give the lives back because they don't have them. . . the child has them and has chosen to give them away by behaving in a certain way.
    ❏ This is an escalation of the previous uses of the three lives technique. If a child loses three lives on three separate occasions there is a further consequence. This will usually involve a more serious sanction and can involve the headteacher and parents.
2. Control techniques – A consistent system of control tactics has to be established, either along the lines of the three lives pattern or a similar approach which can be used by every teacher. Once this is in place there also needs to be smaller-scale techniques that are designed to prevent disruption and stop children behaving in inappropriate ways that need sanctions such as losing lives etc. Both the following techniques can be learnt with practice and they would form a useful part of training and staff development on classroom control techniques.

❏ Technique 1

> Signal of action
> This might be one of a series of usual and common signals which might include: saying a child's name, looking at them and making a signal about what it is that you are concerned with, eg 'Don't shout out. Remember to put up your hand if you want to say something'.

> Move
> As you signal that you intend acting, give further signals such as longer than usual eye contact and move towards the child that you are talking to and whose behaviour is causing concern.

> Take action
> Your intention is to stop something happening to prevent more disruption to your lesson. Stay close to the child, move any distractions and either give quick praise if they have stopped their inappropriate behaviour or take action such as telling them that they have lost a life.

❏ Technique 2

> Signal of action
> Make a clear signal of disapproval such as raised eyebrows and a statement such as: 'Listen to what I am saying and don't talk when I am talking'.

> Specify consequences
> Look at the child as you are talking and make it clear to them what will happen if the behaviour persists, eg 'If you carry on doing that (specify) this will happen (specify)'. This could be simplified to: 'If you do that again you will lose a life. It is your choice'.

Move
Maintain eye contact and move closer to the child, adding a closing comment such as: 'you will remember what I have said won't you'.

Take action
If the inappropriate behaviour persists, you have to take action. You have said what you will do and you now have to do it. But you also have to switch attention back to something different and preferably pleasant. The lesson must go on and disruptive children must realise this.

Body language

This is something that many teachers find amusing or something of a red herring that doesn't apply to them. It is, however, very important. The assertive techniques and styles that have been suggested so far, together with the whole issue of the teaching and learning policy, will not work if any teacher in your school uses inappropriate body language. If they mumble their words or shout all the time, speak too quickly or monotonously, children will stop listening. If they always stand in one place in the classroom without moving around or ignore disruption, children will not have the appropriate boundaries for their behaviour. If they have minimal eye contact and glare at pupils at inappropriate times children will sense a lack of purpose. In fact, to be assertive means linking both verbal and non-verbal signals. Table 7.2 lists some successful techniques that relate to the kind of non-verbal signals that children will recognise.

BASIC CLASSROOM MANAGEMENT SKILLS

Before we look at how it is possible to monitor effective teaching, it is important to complete this section with some idea about what are and are not skills of managing children inside classrooms. Certain aspects of teaching and control styles that have already been discussed in this chapter and in 'The teaching and learning policy' section of Chapter 2 will be relevant, but there are some significant points to make that should be

Table 7.2 *Positive non-verbal techniques*

❏ Confident upright stance.
❏ Firm purposeful movement around the room.
❏ Professional clothes.
❏ Confident smile with direct open eye contact.
❏ Clear and direct eye contact with children you are talking to.
❏ Moving close to children and staying close if it is appropriate.
❏ Using appropriate gestures including raised eyebrows, finger to lips, hand movements etc.
❏ Matching the appropriate non-verbal technique to a spoken statement, eg it is no good leaning on a radiator with a half smile, looking into the distance and reprimanding a child for a bullying incident. Similarly, it is inappropriate to stand with hands on hips, glaring at a child when you are praising their work.

consistently applied in all schools. It is also important to suggest that the teaching styles recommended in the numeracy strategy and the literacy hour will have forced teachers into a way of teaching which should ensure sound classroom management.

Managing a classroom is concerned with how the room is organised, what is actually taught and how. It will be useful for headteachers to emphasise that one of the key characteristics of effective class teachers is their ability to reflect on what they do and how they do it. Developing this reflective and thoughtful approach enables colleagues to learn from their mistakes and develop what has worked well. There are eight sections with sub-headings. Some are longer than others. Once again, they can be part of a series of staff development activities and, as one of the keys to success is self-reflection, two useful questions for headteachers to ask of each of their teachers, and for teachers to ask themselves are: 'Why is it important?' and 'Is it effective'?

1. The beginning of lessons

Lessons need to start on time and there needs to be a clear starting signal. In fact, children need to recognise the same signal over and over again until it becomes automatic. This is extremely helpful because children will know exactly what to do and there will be little if any time wasting. It is also effective if the first part of any lesson follows a pattern that is repeated. This will mean that children know what to expect and how to respond.

The numeracy and literacy strategies are excellent examples of this kind of structured approach.

2. Lesson content

The content of any lesson has to be matched to the ability of the learners and this will involve structured planning which includes differentiated targets for identified children. All schools have policies for curriculum subjects as well as detailed schemes of work which identify what has to be taught, ie the content of lessons. The work set for children should meet the following criteria:

❏ The level is based on previous assessments.
❏ It is the correct level for all children.
❏ It matches individual needs and ensures progression.
❏ It engages children's attention because it is interesting.
❏ It is never too easy, too hard or too repetitious.
❏ It meets the objectives laid down in the school's scheme of work.

3. Planning and preparation

An effective lesson has to be planned thoroughly and there has to be a consistent method of short-, medium- and long-term planning. The medium-term planning will be monitored by the coordinators for specific subjects and is more usually planned with teams of teachers for a period of time such as a half or a full term. Literacy and numeracy, of course, have their own planning structures and schedules. It is the short-term planning that is usually completed each week that is the key to success and raised standards. This is what happens in classrooms. It is based on the content of the medium-term planning but summarises in detail what the teacher is teaching as well as identifying what the children will be learning. Each school should have a consistent method of short-term planning which contains the following:

❏ Enough information for the teacher to know what they are doing at each stage of the lesson.
❏ Identified key objectives which are also told to the children and which indicate what the children will be doing and learning.
❏ Assessment opportunities have also been identified.
❏ Specific resources are identified.

❏ Key learning issues that have caused problems are identified against individual children to inform the next week's short-term planning.

4. Questions and explanations

All teachers need to be able to explain what needs to be learnt and the targets and objectives that are being set. To achieve their aims they also need to be able to ask the right questions of the right children. The success of whole class teaching depends on teachers being able to differentiate their questioning skills to support the learning and progression of children of all levels of ability. They will need to be able to:

❏ use question and answer sessions as a means of giving and receiving information;
❏ include a variety of questions, both open and closed, to involve children of all abilities;
❏ see questioning as a two-way system where children ask questions of each other;
❏ use questions as an assessment tool to find out levels of attainment and to measure understanding and progression.

5. Transition between activities

Let's take the numeracy strategy as an example of what is meant by 'transition between activities'. When the mental whole class activities stop, most teachers will then begin to introduce the main objective of the lesson to the whole class. This means a shift in emphasis and a slight change, which is a time of transition. When the explanation is complete, children start to work in their groups. The change from whole class to group work is a transition which means that children have to move from a tightly controlled situation to one which relies more on their own self-discipline. The final transition occurs when the group work becomes the plenary. Each time that there are changes and shifts in emphasis in the lesson there is the potential for children to behave inappropriately. To prevent this happening teachers need to be able to:

❏ develop transitions that have a smooth, repetitive pattern that children recognise;
❏ ensure that there is no excessive noise or movement between activities;
❏ plan the changes and transitions so that they don't just happen.

6. Behaviour and responses of the children

Classroom management involves discipline and a sense of planned order. All children need to behave well and respond to the work they are doing. Previous sections in this chapter have suggested various teaching strategies and control tactics that are worth introducing into classrooms in a consistent way. Some other broad issues will include:

❑ teachers being aware of everything that is happening in the classroom by moving around the room and being aware of their position in the room in relation to where potentially disruptive children are;
❑ making sure that each child is aware that he or she can be seen by the teacher;
❑ recognising that standing near a child and talking about their work is important;
❑ positive and consistent rules about behaviour are essential in reducing inappropriate behaviour.

7. Teacher attitude

Relationships in the classroom are important. They include how the teacher relates to each child and how children relate to each other. The best attitudes are in classrooms that apply the strategies of being 'firm,' 'fair' and 'consistent'. They will also include such techniques as:

❑ treating each child as an individual and knowing something of their lives out of school;
❑ being approachable and having time to talk;
❑ modelling the kind of behaviour that is expected of children.

8. Ending lessons

If we use the numeracy strategy as an example again, the ending of each numeracy lesson is a drawing together of key issues, reflecting on the objectives that were set at the beginning of the activity, and using examples of children's work to ask further questions that are related to the lesson and to future lessons. Each 'plenary' session in all lessons should be important. Sudden endings are not appropriate. As a summary of these issues we can suggest:

❑ Lessons always end properly and decisively without confusion.
❑ As the lesson draws to a close, the key objectives need to be summarised.
❑ What has been learnt needs to be re-examined during the summary.
❑ Key issues for the next lesson should be introduced.
❑ The end of the lesson is an opportunity to draw the whole class together and to ask appropriate differentiated lessons.

MONITORING THE QUALITY OF TEACHING

There have been many suggestions as to what effective teaching actually is and there will be more in Chapter 9. It is important that all headteachers have evidence about the quality of teaching, and the only way to get this is to observe lessons. Many of these observations will be as a result of performance management but whether this is the only opportunity to watch teachers teach or not, it will only work as part of planned school improvement if everyone understands what the observation process is and how it will work.

Once your school has a teaching and learning policy and there has been some staff development on teaching quality, the next step is to develop a whole staff understanding of lesson observation. Once you have started this process it is important to bear the following in mind:

❑ All successful lesson observation requires preparation and training both for teachers and for the headteacher.
❑ There needs to be a clear understanding on the part of all parties as to why the observation is happening.
❑ Any classroom observation has to have a purpose, eg to monitor phonics teaching, to monitor the use of teaching assistants with SEN children, to find out about how the plenary session in the literacy hour is working etc.
❑ The focus of the observation should be agreed beforehand.
❑ The observer should be as unobtrusive as possible.
❑ The lesson should not be disrupted by the observation and should proceed as smoothly as possible.
❑ After the observation there should be feedback which focuses on what went well and what might be done better or differently next time.
❑ In the case of areas where things might be done better or differently, these could form the basis of targets and objectives within the performance management structure.

Subject observed _____ Date _____

Teacher observed _____

Observer _____

Lesson details	Evaluation
Learning objectives	Were the objectives appropriate for the children? (If not, why not?)
	Were the objectives made clear to the children?
Previous experience of children	
	What assessments were recorded?
Delivery (eg timings, activities, groupings, homework etc)	Were the timings appropriate?
	Were the groupings appropriate?
	Were the activities appropriate?
Resources (eg support staff, materials texts)	Were they differentiated?
	Were high expectations of learning and behaviour maintained?
	Were the resources appropriate?
How effective was this lesson? (very effective/quite effective/ hardly effective/effective in parts)	Why?
Have you a sense of achievement after this lesson? (yes/no)	Why?
Do you feel that the children have a sense of achievement after this lesson? (all/most/some/none)	Why?

Figure 7.2 *Lesson observation, evaluation and feedback form: example 1*

Subject observed _____ Date _____

Teacher observed _____ Observer _____

Learning objectives and assessment (highlight appropriate comments) Appropriate/not appropriate/lack of clarity/shared/not shared/reinforced/ not reinforced/achieved/not achieved/ partly achieved/assessments recorded/ not recorded	Comments
Delivery OK/issue Exposition OK/issue Question and answer OK/issue Reinforcement OK/issue Praise OK/issue Activities OK/issue Pace OK/issue Pupils on task OK/issue Teacher–pupil interaction OK/issue Groupings OK/issue Teacher mobility OK/issue Timings OK/issue Overall structure of the lesson OK/issue Marking OK/issue Health and safety OK/issue	Comments
Resources Arrangement of furniture OK/issue Availablility of resources OK/issue Quality and suitability of resources OK/issue	Comments
Relationships Order and class control OK/issue Attitude of children OK/issue Adaptability OK/issue	Comments Comments
Suggestions for future lessons	

Figure 7.3 *Lesson observation, evaluation and feedback form: example 2*

Subject observed _____ Date _____

Teacher observed _____ Observer _____

TEACHING

Teaching input (What is the teacher doing?)	Impact on children (What are the children doing as a result of the teaching?)

LEARNING

What evidence is there of pupils learning and making progress? Three agreed points about the lesson Two agreed areas for future development

Figure 7.4 *Lesson observation, evaluation and feedback form: example 3*

There is no best way of recording observations. Each school will have its own preferences and many LEAs will also provide examples through their inspectors' links with school. Ofsted also have their own lesson observation, which is usually thought to be too judgemental for use in most schools. Figures 7.2, 7.3 and 7.4 suggest three different forms that could be used to observe lessons and monitor the performance of teachers. Each one has its strengths and it is up to individual schools to take decisions as to which one they will find to be the most effective.

IMPORTANT POINTS

This chapter can be linked to several others. Chapter 2 discusses the teaching and learning policy, Chapter 8 will suggest ways that the curriculum and subject coordinators influence what happens in the classroom and Chapter 9 will use some of Ofsted's criteria for what is and is not an effective way of working. What happens in the classroom is at the centre of raising standards and teaching quality should be part of the School Development Plan and part of each individual teacher's performance management targets:

❏ Headteachers must monitor the quality of teaching throughout the school.
❏ They must also know what high-quality teaching actually looks like and take steps to include it in training and staff development programmes.
❏ Teachers have to be able to demonstrate that they are effective professionals in the classroom.
❏ All teacher need to be assertive and not aggressive or passive in their relationships with children and in their teaching styles.
❏ Teachers are in control and must have a range of control tactics that work with all their children.
❏ As well as using control tactics, teachers must also be capable of using a range of styles which fits into a consistent way of working with children.

DEVELOPING CURRICULUM MANAGERS AND CURRICULUM POLICIES

When leadership was discussed in Chapter 6 and when the school as an organisation was evaluated in Chapter 4, the role of curriculum or subject coordinator (often known as the curriculum manager) was raised as a vital part of the school's management structure. Chapter 3 also began a brief evaluation of the role of a curriculum coordinator in relation to the whole staff team. In fact, if a large amount of the work surrounding different subjects of the National Curriculum is not delegated then the school will not only cease to function effectively, it will stop working at all. The spread of work has to be between colleagues who take their share of managing a particular curriculum area and the subsequent teaching and learning. There are many reasons why headteachers have to organise their schools by delegating to colleagues some managerial responsibilities. One of the main ones is that it is impossible for every teacher to keep up with every change in every primary curriculum subject. They will certainly need to have some knowledge of how curriculum changes might affect their planning, teaching and assessment but they cannot be experts in everything. Making sure that one colleague has, as their role, a certain expertise and overview of a specific curriculum area will make sure that colleagues know that there is someone to turn to for advice and support.

MAIN REASONS FOR SCHOOLS TO HAVE CURRICULUM COORDINATORS

Of course, each primary coordinator should not be seen as the ultimate 'expert'. That would be impossible in small schools where one person may be coordinating several subjects. Their broad overview of a particular area must include an involvement in staff development training and they must take the lead in the formation of policies and schemes of work. In other words, they must be capable of leading other teachers and developing good practice. The fact that headteachers cannot manage schools without delegation applies equally to curriculum coordinators. They must make sure that colleagues are aware of the following implications of how a coordinator's role might be seen to work:

❏ Coordination is a key task in all primary schools but it can only raise standards if all teachers continue to collaborate and work together with each coordinator.

❏ There has to be a whole school ethos of supportive colleagues in order to create a coherent curriculum that is consistently followed by all teachers. This will mean that the headteacher has a major role of coordinating the coordinators to make sure that there is a consistency of approach.

❏ The headteacher is responsible for the actions of those teachers to whom he or she has delegated tasks, jobs and initiatives. It is important that everyone is clear about how much responsibility and authority is delegated as well as how much support will be given to each coordinator by both the headteacher and deputy and all teacher colleagues.

❏ All coordinators will need support both in the kind of staff development that they need and in dealing with all the trials and tribulations that arise out of leading meetings and managing change.

❏ Time is a key factor in whether a coordinator is able to be as effective as they would like. Each headteacher will have to deal with this within the context of their own schools, but there is a need for coordinators to have non-contact time, release for daytime courses and some secretarial support.

Table 8.1 suggests some of the questions that headteachers need to ask about what curriculum coordinators do and how they are able to do the job that has been asked of them. (There is a similar list in Chapter 3.)

It should be obvious, from both the direction of the questions in Table 8.1 and what the answers are telling you, that it is very important for any curriculum coordinator to be able to provide leadership and direction for their subject and to ensure that it is managed and organised in such a way that it meets the aims and objectives of the school. To do this properly, they will need time to talk to colleagues and time to work alongside them and observe them teaching. This, of course, means time out of the classroom, cover from a supply teacher and all the associated costs. But, if school improvement and raising standards are important to the headteacher and

Table 8.1 *Questions about the role of coordinators*

❑ How long has each curriculum coordinator had oversight of their particular subject?
❑ Have they each got a job description that reflects their responsibilities?
❑ Are they monitoring the medium- and short-term planning of other teachers in their subject?
❑ How are they able to influence the work of their colleagues?
❑ Are all coordinators able to do any joint planning with other teachers?
❑ Are subject coordinators able to observe colleagues teaching?
❑ Do they have any non-contact time?
❑ How do they get an overview of standards in their subject?
❑ Is the policy statement for each subject up to date?
❑ Are there assessment, recording and reporting arrangements in place for each subject?
❑ How much budget is allocated to each coordinator?
❑ How are resource needs identified?
❑ Are the needs of the subject reflected in the School Development Plan and individual teachers' performance management targets?
❑ Do subject coordinators run training and staff development sessions in school?

to the governors, it would be counterproductive not to make it clear to all coordinators, and this may mean all teachers in small schools, that for them to do their job properly they will be given some time away from their 'normal' teaching duties.

A COORDINATOR'S OVERALL RESPONSIBILITIES

An effective subject coordinator has to have the delegated responsibility for securing high standards as well as playing a major role in the development of school policy and practice. They will also play a key role in the following:

❑ guiding and motivating teachers;
❑ evaluating the effectiveness of both teaching and learning;
❑ setting appropriate targets for their subject which have been identified in the School Development Plan;

❑ identifying needs within the subject;
❑ matching subject needs against those of the whole school;
❑ understanding how their subject contributes to the priorities of the whole school;
❑ understanding how their subject contributes to the overall education and achievement of all children.

Bell (1992) looked at the most common jobs carried out by primary coordinators and suggested that there were 10 key tasks which are listed in rank order in Table 8.2. It is possible to classify the list under four broad headings:

1. those areas concerned with subject development;
2. areas concerned with supporting colleagues as they teach the subject;
3. evaluating the teaching and learning that takes place in the subject;
4. evaluating the impact the teaching is having on the standards achieved and the progress that is being made.

Table 8.2 *Common tasks carried out by subject coordinators (in rank order)*

1. Communicating with the headteacher
2. Exercising curricular leadership
3. Communicating with staff
4. Organising resources
5. Establishing and maintaining continuity and consistency throughout the school
6. Organising training and staff development
7. Liaising between head and staff
8. Establishing recording systems
9. Motivating staff
10. Engaging in curriculum development

POSSIBLE DIFFICULTIES IN GETTING THE JOB DONE

Reading the list of activities and tasks that a subject coordinator has to get to grips with should suggest that the job is immense and very difficult to complete effectively. The immensity of the task is also increased by several possible constraints that are experienced by most, if not all, schools. It is important that the coordinators themselves as well as the headteacher and senior teachers get to grips with such constraints so that the frustrations of not being able to do their job properly does not minimise the effect coordinators have on raising standards.

Personal confidence

There are many reasons why responsibility for a subject, or sometimes several in a primary school, can cause a fall in confidence. It may be related to a lack of expertise in a particular subject which needs to be tackled by more training or some concerns about the coordinator's interpersonal skills such as leadership, chair of meetings etc. If this is the case, it is very important that the headteacher and other senior teachers are seen to support their colleagues and minimise the effect this kind of lack in confidence can have on the individual and on colleagues.

Problems related to clarifying tasks and prioritising

This is very similar to identifying key issues in the School Development Plan. Once a task has been allocated and is owned by a specific coordinator, they will have to break the job down into its smaller component parts.

Clemson (1996) suggested how this could be done and Figure 8.1 is a modification of this. There are only five tasks in this example. In a coordinator's real world, there would be many more.

The chart is really an attempt to break down the role into more manageable chunks and the coordinator will have to use the headings to allocate tasks, parts of tasks, or just use it as an aide-mémoire to identify who needs to be involved in any discussions that are taking place.

Relationships with colleagues

This is a difficult issue, and what makes it worse is that it is relatively common for the work of coordinators to be frustrated by colleagues whose personal behaviour interferes with what should be a professional relationship. Problems and frustrations can arise because of personality clashes, differences in values and conflicts related to status (this is more commonly found when young teacher coordinators have to exert their influence on older, more 'experienced' colleagues).

Task	SMT	Head	Coordinator	All staff	Misc. notes
Organise and manage groups to write subject policy					
Ensure equal opportunity					
Evaluate classroom practice in teaching the subject					
Keep records of pupil progress					
Plan and provide staff development opportunities for colleagues					

Figure 8.1 *Allocation of roles and responsibilities for a coordinator*

Time and resources

Lack of time in relation to a coordinator's other roles as class teacher, for example, has always been a real issue that is extremely difficult to solve but needs to be managed in some way. It is also true that budgetary constraints have meant that resource provision has barely been adequate. Both these areas will benefit from a whole school approach which is seen to balance time and resource provision and allocation fairly.

Delegation

Curriculum responsibilities have to be delegated or the school will not be able to function effectively. Headteachers have to be comfortable with this delegation and have to feel that the delegated tasks will be carried out effectively. Harrison and Gill (1992), in *Primary School Management*, argue that how successful delegated responsibilities will be will depend to a large extent on how far the school has developed in the following areas:

❑ how confident curriculum coordinators feel in making decisions without having to ask, meet and wait for top down agreement from the headteacher;

❑ whether there is a system of team leaders, including the head, who know how to monitor the work of coordinators together with the whole structure of what they are doing and how it is linked to the school development plan and the raising of standards;

❑ the degree to which there is consideration of personal needs and the circumstances under which coordinators are working, especially in such areas as time and any conflicts that may need resolving;

❑ how well developed the structures that maintain the roles of curriculum coordinator are, for example class release time, training and opportunities for the coordinator to monitor teaching quality;

❑ whether coordinators are seen as models of good practice in their subject and whether headteachers are also models of how the relationships between colleagues actually work;

❑ the degree to which coordinators are able to work in harmony with the school's ethos and stated aims.

THE EFFECT SUCCESSFUL SUBJECT LEADERSHIP WILL HAVE ON THE SCHOOL

It is obvious from previous sections that a skilful subject coordinator will have a positive effect on both teachers and children. It is also the case, however, that they will also have an impact on parents, teaching assistants and how the headteacher and deputy head manage the school. There is a much fuller list of the skills and attributes of a coordinator in the TTA publication (1998) *National Standards for Subject Leaders* in what has become known in schools as the 'Rainbow pack', but all of the following skills have to be taken into consideration:

❑ **The coordinator and the children** – If a subject is coordinated well, it should mean that the content of lessons is carefully planned and that the teaching is well organised and effective. Children will show improvements in how they understand the subject and they will show that they have progressed in relation to their previous attainments. They will also be interested in the subject and enthusiastic about it, and this enthusiasm and hard work will help teachers maintain a purposeful working atmosphere in their classrooms.

❏ **The coordinator and other teachers** – An effective coordinator will want to build up teams of teachers who are able to teach the subject in a consistent and successful way using policies and schemes of work that they have played a part in writing and developing. Not only will they be motivated by the coordinator to teach well, but they will be enthusiastic about motivating children and be able to set challenging and realistic targets that are based on a sound knowledge of what each child is capable of achieving. By being motivated to teach the subject well, everyone will want to maximise their knowledge by making good use of any training that is offered that will support their expertise. They will also be encouraged by an effective coordinator to make use of appropriate teaching and learning approaches as well as selecting new resources to meet the learning objectives of their class.

❏ **The coordinator and parents** – When parents are kept well informed about their child's progress and achievements and their probable future targets, they are more likely to be supportive of the school's wider achievements.

❏ **The coordinator and the headteacher and other senior teachers** – If a subject coordinator is successful they will make sure that all senior managers are well briefed about their subject. They will also go beyond this and see that they also understand what they have achieved, what they are doing to make sure they meet the deadlines of their perform-ance management targets as well as their tasks within the School Development Plan.

❏ **The coordinator and teaching assistants** – A good coordinator will not waste the time and talents of teaching assistants. They will make sure that they are well briefed, trained within the classroom and that they understand what has to be done with specifically targeted children. By doing this, they will make sure that teaching assistants are a vital part of the teaching and learning process and that they are able to support the teachers in their classrooms.

Another way of looking at and trying to come to terms with what curric-ulum coordinators should do to be effective is to see much of what is involved in their work as a series of changes. Curriculum coordinators have to be able to manage change. Gadsby and Harrison (1999) in *The Primary Coordinator and Ofsted Reinspection* suggest that there are six categories that will help coordinators not only to be more effective, but to be seen to be successful by their colleagues. They are summarised in Table 8.3.

Table 8.3 *Skills to help coordinators to be more effective*

Challenge	Help colleagues see changes in a specific subject as a challenge and not as a threat.
Communicate	Keep colleagues informed about the subject, including school initiatives, local and national initiatives and any training opportunities and results of any internal monitoring.
Commitment	The more colleagues are involved in the change and in implementing it, in other words, the more they 'own' the subject, the more committed they will be to make their teaching and learning effective.
Control	It is important for colleagues not to feel powerless in the face of changes to specific subjects. They need to participate in changes and new initiatives and they also need to have a certain amount of control by being able to implement the course of any change that affects them.
Confidence	Each coordinator needs to build up the confidence of colleagues so that they feel good about teaching each subject and feel competent that what they are doing is having a positive effect on learning and that standards are being raised.
Connect	Meetings with coordinators from other schools is always useful and will always boost confidence. It will also help individual coordinators keep up to date with changes and initiatives.

THE SCHOOL'S CURRICULUM VISION

It is important before we go any further to begin to identify what is actually meant by 'the curriculum'. Let's start with a statement from the *Handbook for Inspecting Primary and Nursery Schools* (Ofsted, 1999) which applies to a very good to excellent school. They suggest that: ' The curriculum interprets statutory requirements in a stimulating as well as structured ways, providing for high achievement, particularly in core subjects, and offering pupils a wealth of additional opportunities' (p 66).

The phrase 'statutory requirements' suggests a core of knowledge which, as we now know, belongs to the state and has, as one of its aims, to be broad as well as balanced. Another cliché is that the curriculum is: 'everything that happens in an organised way in the school'.

Whatever our interpretation of what is being taught, it is important for colleagues within the same school to share a curriculum vision which has been carefully thought through and discussed. Table 8.4 identifies the three stages in developing a shared curriculum vision.

Table 8.4 *Three stages in developing the curriculum*

Stage 1	Identify the priorities for a particular curriculum area. Examine what is currently happening.
Stage 2	Identify what children actually need to: ❑ learn; ❑ be able to do; ❑ know and understand; ❑ have thought about.
Stage 3	Plan the revised curriculum so that the learning outcomes are met through existing and new curriculum opportunities.

What is the curriculum?

As soon as it is obvious that there need to be changes to how the curriculum operates, it should also become apparent that questions about the current provision need to be asked. The three most basic questions that headteachers and other senior managers, including curriculum coordinators, need to ask are:

❑ How is the curriculum taught?
❑ What teaching styles are used?
❑ How is the curriculum managed?

Fortunately, all three questions have been recognised already and each one has been part of the content of earlier chapters. What hasn't been considered is the importance of the curriculum as the public face of the school. This will include the 'subjects', the classroom teaching styles and the content. When trying to identify these areas of the curriculum there seems to be at least five relatively common characteristics:

❑ **Breadth** – There seems to be higher achievement in basic skills if there is a wide range of subjects and extra curricular activities.
❑ **Balance** – An appropriate weight of time needs to be given to different aspects of the curriculum. This was recognised in *Curriculum Organisation and Classroom Practice in Primary Schools: A Follow up Report* (DfEE,

1993) when it was suggested that: 'If schools were over stretched to provide the National Curriculum, depth was likely to be sacrificed in pursuit of breadth. The aim should be to strike a better balance than currently existed which meant attempting less but doing it more thoroughly' (1993: 15–16).

❏ **Relevance** – What children learn in school needs to be recognised by children as having some relevance. All children need to know why they are learning things and it is important that they understand the objectives behind lessons.

❏ **Differentiation** – What is taught has to be matched to the needs of each class as well as to individual children. Teachers need to be aware of the need to differentiate as well as to challenge children at the most appropriate level. This match of task to ability will mean that what is taught should be learnt more effectively.

❏ **Progression and continuity** – The primary curriculum from the foundation stages to the end of Year 6 needs to be seen as a whole. It is important that teachers have an overview of all the stages in their own school.

A management policy to support the vision

In one sense, a policy is an agreement that everyone in the school has entered into. There is a belief that the processes of writing the policy should involve as many teachers as possible because by 'owning' the policy, they are more likely to have a stake in it and are, therefore, more likely to adhere to what it says about individual subjects. If a policy fails, it is more than likely to be because those teachers who are supposed to implement it were not consulted when it was being discussed, drafted and passed for whole school use. The main aims for a policy can be identified fairly simply and it will be useful for coordinators to realise that, although the policy for their subject is important, it is possible to summarise the effect it will have on the whole school using a small number of bullet points:

❏ The policy demonstrates the school's intentions for children's learning in a subject.
❏ It gives information to teachers, parents, governors and inspectors.
❏ It provides a framework for planning what is being taught.
❏ It helps continuity and progression as well as establishing continuity within the subject.

Whatever curriculum subject a coordinator is working in and whatever curriculum is being planned will depend to a large extent on several key management issues being identified and implemented. These issues are not, however, just the province of headteachers and senior managers. All teachers need to be in agreement with them. They will include:

❏ **Entitlement** – Everyone needs to agree that all children are entitled to a curriculum that can draw on their individual talents.
❏ **Consensus** – There has to be consensus that the curriculum can be resourced in terms of teachers' time, training and the necessary resources.
❏ **Professionalism** – Professional control over the content of the curriculum has largely been taken away from teachers and they have been left with interpreting a nationally laid down curriculum framework. Coordinators have to motivate staff to identify what their children need and what they need to teach.
❏ **Responsiveness** – Success in teaching is partly dependent on recognising that the curriculum needs to start from the child's own knowledge, that is, where a child is at a particular time and place. Teachers need to be able to respond to the needs of the children they teach within the breadth and balance of their curriculum.

A FRAMEWORK FOR THE WHOLE SCHOOL CURRICULUM POLICY AND FOR INDIVIDUAL SUBJECT POLICIES

Of course, as the leader of curriculum coordinators, it is the responsibility of the headteacher to consider what it is that you want to teach (remember the National Curriculum is not the whole curriculum) and what you expect the children to learn and achieve. There are several ways in which this might happen. They are included in Smith (2001) *Making Your School More Successful: Pack 1* and summarised in Table 8.5. These aspects of any structured curriculum are learning processes, that is, the how of what has to be taught rather than the content of what has to be learnt. In many ways, the areas listed in Table 8.5 are universal and apply to all schools, whereas 'what has to be learnt' can be arranged in many different ways, including single subjects for each curriculum area at one end and multi-subject themes with a single subject focus.

Broad whole school curriculum statement

Each school needs to have a curriculum policy which is a broad statement of intent rather than a policy for a specific subject. An example of such a

Table 8.5 *The curriculum must develop achievement in the following areas*

Academic attainment	Children must be able to read, write and respond appropriately, remember facts without having to look everything up and organise the material that they are using.
Applying knowledge	Children must be able to deal with the practical as well as theoretical knowledge and the spoken as well as the written word. Problem solving and investigational skills are important when applying knowledge.
Social and interpersonal skills	This is the capacity to communicate with others face-to-face and the ability to cooperate with them. It is about initiative, self-reliance and the ability to work alone without being closely supervised.
Motivation and commitment	This is about persevering, learning in spite of difficulties and being willing to try new things.
Decision making and independent thinking	Individual children need to be able to exercise choice, take decisions and express their own points of view.
Equal opportunities	The curriculum will expect all children to adopt a positive attitude towards a multiracial society as well as learning to appreciate other people's right to be different.

statement is in Figure 8.2 and summarises a similar statement in Smith (2000) *Meeting the Challenges of Curriculum 2000*. This is not a definitive statement but it can be used as a starting point in most schools. This is important, because such an important, yet general statement should ideally be agreed with the whole staff and, as an initiative, it will be more than likely led by the headteacher or deputy head.

The narrower specific subject curriculum

A curriculum policy for a specific subject is a statement which sets out the general framework and teaching and learning approach to the subject. While it does reflect the views of the school's whole curriculum statement, it narrows down the focus significantly and develops the framework for an individual subject. Within the school it is the curriculum coordinator's

---

In this school we aim to deliver a high-quality education to all children.

We will do this by providing a well-balanced curriculum which will be:

❑ broad and balanced based on the requirements of the National Curriculum;
❑ stimulating and challenging in a way that will extend children's knowledge, skills and creativity in order to develop enquiring minds;
❑ committed to the principle of equality for all children;
❑ relevant to the needs and interests of all children;
❑ able to provide all children with the skills to develop their potential intellectually, physically and emotionally;
❑ able to allow each child to question, acquire self-knowledge and develop independence;
❑ able to provide children with the opportunity to develop their own self-esteem.

The curriculum will be taught using a variety of teaching styles and groupings, as appropriate to the intellectual and emotional development of the needs of the children.

All children will be provided with opportunities to learn from a wide range of experiences.

All teaching will be planned to develop individuals' potential and will take account of both previous and future learning needs.

Children will have regular and constructive feedback about their work.

All children will, commensurate with their ability and maturity, be expected to evaluate their work and social relationships in order to improve personal standards and enhance relationships.

Figure 8.2 *The whole school curriculum statement*

responsibility to present draft ideas to a larger working party but it is the head's job to see that the policy is in line with the school's ethos and is one that will be scrutinised by the governors and passed back to the school as a document which is accepted by everyone and which will move the school forward. The following areas are likely to be included in each of your subject's curriculum policy statements:

❑ a statement which recognises the unique elements of the specific subject;
❑ curriculum aims that are specific to the subject;

❏ specific links to the National Curriculum programmes of study where this is appropriate;
❏ ways in which curriculum activities are planned;
❏ the principles and methods by which the subject is taught (this will relate to the teaching and learning policy as described in Chapter 2);
❏ how continuity and progression in the teaching and learning of the subject will be achieved;
❏ how the teaching in the subject will be differentiated to meet the needs of all children, including those with special educational needs;
❏ how records will be kept and assessments made;
❏ how resources will be allocated and shared;
❏ how equal opportunities will be guaranteed;
❏ how the policy will be monitored and evaluated and within what time-scale.

The most important area for headteachers to be involved in is recognising and agreeing that individual policies say what the subject is about and what the important principles are for teaching and learning. There is no doubt that each subject policy is likely to be slightly similar, but it is also true that there will be important generic differences that each coordinator will introduce into the policies for their subjects.

CHARACTERISTICS OF AN EFFECTIVE POLICY STATEMENT

It should have become obvious that each school will have different views about what are and are not the characteristics of a policy that actually works. In some schools, for example, everything will be in place within a structure of policy development, monitor and evaluate, and rewrite. In other schools the processes which are needed to create effective policies are being developed, and many policies are needing to be developed. In delegating tasks to coordinators it is important to make sure that they recognise that they will need to take the lead in drafting policies and schemes of work for their subject. They will need to be leaders and will be subject to all the difficulties and frustrations that leaders face in terms of time management and stress avoidance. How easy or difficult their role is will depend to a considerable extent on how both the ethos and leadership of the school create the kind of relationships that promote successful team building and decision making. Table 8.6 summarises some of the characteristics of an effective policy statement but it also depends on the following assumptions which can equally apply when coordinators are also taking the lead in developing schemes of work:

❑ The school has working parties and teams to support and help coordinators.
❑ Those in the teams will be able to support coordinators through their knowledge of teaching the subject under consideration.
❑ An action plan and structure will be needed for the team.
❑ Having a real and realistic deadline is important and it is also essential to try and stick to it.
❑ There needs to be a system where other teachers, the head and governors are consulted at appropriate times during the development of the policy or scheme of work and are given the opportunity to make comments that are taken on board and which might affect the content of the policy.

Table 8.6 *Characteristics of an effective policy*

1. All teachers in the school are committed to making the policy work because they were involved to some degree in developing and writing it.
2. The reason for writing the policy is not just that it is part of the School Development Plan, but that it will focus teaching and learning, raise standards and be part of the school's focus on continuous improvement.
3. It needs to be clearly written, as jargon-free as possible and clear in stating what has to be done within the subject.
4. There need to be clear guidelines on actions that need to be taken and how certain things will be done.
5. How the policy will be monitored and evaluated needs to be built in.
6. The policy should be written for a specific audience and it should be as brief as possible as well as being easily understood.

THE POLICY AND THE SCHEME OF WORK

Each scheme of work must be subject-based and must identify which parts of the curriculum, including the National Curriculum, must be taught to each year group and to each class. Each coordinator will have to divide up the curriculum so that teachers know exactly what to plan to teach and by doing this there can be continuity and very little unplanned repetition. The scheme of work for a subject has to provide guidelines about what should be learnt and should also set out clear learning outcomes so that teachers have something against which they can assess learning outcomes. If the headteacher and the coordinator support clear policies and schemes of work that are detailed but not overwhelmingly prescriptive, then each individual teacher's short-term planning becomes their creative interpretation of detailed curriculum areas. Rather than describing the curriculum in a variety of different ways, a consistent approach to curriculum policies and schemes of work will also mean a consistent approach to planning, which helps raise attainment because objectives and teaching aims are always clear from class to class and year group to year group. Gadsby and Harrison (1999), in *The Primary Co-ordinator and Ofsted Re-inspection*, emphasise the importance of schemes of work when they suggest: 'The scheme of work can be critical in providing the subject information necessary if non-specialists are to implement curriculum policy and the scheme of work effectively' (p 99).

The whole point of a coordinator developing a scheme of work is to make it easier for colleagues to translate curriculum policy into practice. An effective scheme of work will also mean that balance, continuity and progression are more easily secured and more easily measured because there is a document against which such values can be measured. Table 8.7 identifies some characteristics of an effective scheme of work and the suggestion is that if each coordinator does have a policy and scheme of work in place, then it is more likely that the school will have a 'quality' curriculum.

Table 8.7 *Characteristics of an effective scheme of work*

1. Teachers are able to get out of each scheme of work exactly what they have to teach in the subject.
2. The scheme of work identifies how much time is available.
3. The content of the scheme of work has to be linked to the National Curriculum programmes of study.
4. The content of each subject is divided into both clear learning objectives and clear learning activities.
5. It will identify teaching approaches as well as resources.
6. It is important that schemes of work are not seen to be tablets of stone, but can be easily modified and changed.
7. Effective schemes of work will allow children to progress through the subject in a way that builds on earlier learning.

TIME AVAILABLE FOR THE PLANNED CURRICULUM

It is an appropriate ending to this chapter to look at examples of the time that is available for teaching together with the problems this introduces into the structure of the school year and, by a process of reduction, into the school week and the school day. The idea of breaking down the day, week and year into time slots is also partly related to what was known, when it was introduced into the pay and conditions of service of teachers, as directed time; that is, the time for teachers to work that can be directed by the headteacher. There are two examples of how the amount of curriculum time to be allocated can be identified. Figure 8.3 is for the Infant age range and Figure 8.4 for Juniors. It is an important distinction because the time committed to teaching National Curriculum subjects, RE and other curricular provision can be shorter for Infant children.

Obviously each subject has an allocated period of time for the year and for the week, and each school should include this in their curriculum statement. It is important for headteachers and curriculum coordinators to make sure that each subject is allocated an appropriate amount of time and that the time is used well. The only way to do this is to have clear policies for each subject, detailed schemes of work, a consistent whole school planning policy and, of course, very clear and positive teaching and learning styles. If we use the times from Figures 8.3 and 8.4, a breakdown of each area of the curriculum into hours each year and hours each week would look like Tables 8.8 and 8.9.

To say that curriculum time is short would be an understatement. The amount of time taken up by the core subjects is more than half the hours available for teaching each week. This puts pressure on coordinators to make sure that all other curriculum areas are covered effectively and the coordinators of the core subjects will have to make sure that the use of such a large amount of time is fully justified. Playfoot *et al* (1989), in *The Primary School Management Book*, make the point that to make this happen coordinators have to have a sense of direction and be persistent. They suggest that, 'The person leading the change (curriculum coordinator) needs to be visible, working with their "sleeves rolled up", touring, talking, making practical adjustments, listening and leading. . .' (1989: 73).

The idea of shared responsibility is important and the quality of the coordinator's leadership is important and, at the same time, needs support from both the headteacher and colleagues.

Both Elliott and Kemp (1983) and Rogers (1980) suggest that effective leaders, and this will obviously include subject coordinators, have many of the following characteristics:

Sessions in the school day 8.55am–12 noon (3 hrs 5 mins)
1.00pm–3.20pm (2 hrs 20 mins)

Total time in school 5 hrs 25 mins per day
27 hrs 5 mins per week

Breaks (playtimes) 2 hrs 30 mins per week

Assembly/collective worship 1 hr 15 mins per week

Registration 1 hr per week

Time committed to teaching National Curriculum subjects, RE and other curricular provision 22 hrs 20 mins per week

Number of weeks available during the school year 38 weeks (+5 training days)

Special curriculum events and activities which require short blocks of time planned within the appropriate term for individual year groups
2 weeks
For example:
 End of key stage tests
 Residential visits
 Christmas parties
 Rehearsals
 Sports days
 Links with the local community
 Book week

Remaining weeks committed to teaching the school curriculum 36 weeks

Total number of hours 804 hours

Statutory curriculum provision: KS1 programmes of study for all National Curriculum subjects, RE and PSHE

Figure 8.3 *Curriculum time allocation for Infant classes*

Sessions in the school day: 8.55am–12.15pm (3 hrs 20 mins)
  1.15pm–3.20pm (2 hrs 5 mins)

Total time in school 5 hrs 25 mins per day
  27 hrs 5 mins per week

Breaks (maximum with some pm not taken) 2 hrs 5 mins per week

Assembly/collective worship 1 hour per week

Registration 45 mins per week

Time committed to teaching National Curriculum subjects, RE and other curricular provision 23 hrs 15 mins per week

Number of weeks available during school year 38 weeks (+ 5 training days)

Special curriculum events and activities which require short blocks of time planned within the appropriate term for individual year groups
For example:
  End of key stage tests
  Residential visits
  Christmas parties
  Rehearsals
  Sports days
  Links with local community
  Book week

Remaining weeks committed to teaching the school curriculum 36 weeks

Total 837 hours

Statutory curriculum provision KS2 programmes of study for all NC subjects , RE and PSHE

Figure 8.4 *Curriculum time allocation for Junior classes*

Table 8.8 *Infant curriculum time breakdown*

SUBJECT	HOURS PER YEAR	HOURS PER WEEK
English	210	5.84
Maths	180	5
Science	63	1 .75
Design and Technology	36	1
ICT	48	1.33
History	36	1
Geography	36	1
Art and Design	36	1
Music	36	1
PE	72	2
Modern F.L.	0	0
RE	27	0.75
PSHE	24	0.66
Total	804	22 hrs. 20 mins.

Table 8.9 *Junior curriculum time break down (Year 5. There are slight variations between Y3/4 and Y5/6)*

SUBJECT	HOURS PER YEAR	HOURS PER WEEK
English	208	5.75
Maths	180	5
Science	80	2.25
Design and Technology	36	1
ICT	36	1
History	36	1
Geography	36	1
Art and Design	36	1
Music	36	1
PE	72	2
Modern F.L.	27	0.75
RE	27	0.75
PSHE	27	0.75
Total	837	23 hrs. 15 mins.

❑ **Self awareness** – Being aware of their own attitudes and values and how they affect other people.
❑ **Will to achieve** – They will always want to seek new challenges.
❑ **Optimism** – They will feel positive about the future and their part in it.
❑ **Positive regard** – They will respond to others with warmth and respect.
❑ **Trust** – This is the extent to which we are prepared to place trust in those colleagues who work with us.
❑ **Congruence** – This is the security we feel in working alongside colleagues.
❑ **Empathy** – They will need to be good at understanding others' points of view.
❑ **Courage** – This is the ability to take risks to find more effective ways of working with colleagues.

IMPORTANT POINTS

One of the key tasks of leadership and also one of the most difficult to manage is delegation. But delegating work to colleagues is essential because headteachers and deputy headteachers cannot manage the whole curriculum. It is an impossibility, and curriculum coordinators have to take on key leadership roles for specific subject areas. They must have some expertise as well as an overview of a curriculum area which will include policy development as well as the creation of an agreed scheme of work:

❑ Subject coordination is about managing an area of the curriculum to raise standards as part of the school's development and improvement plan.
❑ It is important for coordinators to work alongside colleagues and to observe lessons in their specific subject.
❑ Under the overall leadership of the headteacher, they must be able to guide and motivate colleagues, set appropriate targets and identify specific needs for the subject they are responsible for, as well as being in a position to influence what happens in the classroom in terms of teaching and learning.
❑ A curriculum coordinator faces considerable difficulties, which range from personal areas such as lack of confidence, prioritising tasks and managing the time available to negative relationships with colleagues.
❑ The principle aim of effective subject coordination should be to raise standards by having a positive influence on children, colleagues, headteacher, teaching assistants, governors and parents.

❏ Everything they do should be linked to the need to develop a broad, balanced, relevant and differentiated curriculum within the boundaries of the ethos and culture of the school.

❏ There needs to be a broad-based whole school curriculum plan together with policies and schemes of work for each individual subject.

❏ The most effective policies and schemes of work that influence practice and raise standards will have been created with the involvement of the whole staff, including the headteachers and preferably governors.

❏ There is a limited amount of teaching time available during the school week and the school year. Its use needs to be carefully organised and managed.

MANAGING A SUCCESSFUL INSPECTION

By now all schools will have had their first inspection and for many, the joys of the second will still be embedded in their collective memory. This is the final chapter and it is likely to contain some elements of previous sections of other chapters. The reason for this is that we are all conscious of the expectations that Ofsted have. Knowing what Ofsted expect will mean that their requirements, their demands and their standards, when related to quality, will be part of everything that every primary school plans and manages. It would be a brave and probably suicidal headteacher who decided to ignore any of the guidelines that are available from Ofsted. Having said that, many of the chapters in this book have sections in them that are related in some way to some of Ofsted's criteria. Chapter 4, for example, has a long section which discusses the involvement of governors in the inspection process. It would be an equally crazy author who, at the same time as wanting to write a book which suggests and discusses good practice, totally ignored an area of expertise which, whilst feared rather than liked, has many areas of recommended good practice.

The Ofsted (1999) publication, *Inspecting Schools: Handbook for Inspecting Primary and Nursery Schools*, is a thorough and detailed summary of their expectations. This chapter will draw on that, as have other chapters, but rather then repeat what can easily be read and discussed in Ofsted publications there will be other areas which headteachers and schools might find useful in their preparation for an inspection or in their reflection on an inspection that has just taken place.

INSPECTION SUMMARY

Over a four-year cycle (which has now been extended to six years), schools will be inspected in order to identify their strengths and weaknesses. This, according to Ofsted, will help them to improve the quality of the education they provide for children and raise the standards achieved. All schools will receive a short or full inspection within the cycle and the criteria for selecting a school for a short inspection are related to judgements from the school's previous inspection and data from the school's PANDA. Schools selected will have been judged good, very good or excellent in the quality of education, ethos, leadership and management. The PANDA will need to show C or better in all core subjects and the trend data that is available will need to show improving standards at least in line with or better than the national trend.

Short and full inspections will have many common features, including:

❑ Evidence from documentation, observation and consultation.
❑ They will report on standards, quality and efficiency.
❑ The team will include a lay inspector.
❑ They can both lead to a judgement of serious weaknesses or special measures.
❑ The report will include the current standard summary for parents.

The differences between short and full inspections will include:

❑ Only a full inspection will include a report on all subjects.
❑ All teachers may not be observed in short inspections.
❑ Short inspections will be issues-led based on pre-inspection evidence.

The inspection of *your* school (and this *'your'* is important in terms of headteachers being held accountable) will ask the following eight questions:

1. What sort of school is it?
2. How high are standards?
3. How well are children taught?
4. How good are curricular and other opportunities?
5. How well does the school care for its children?
6. How well does the school work in partnership with its parents and carers?
7. How well is the school led and managed?
8. What should the school do to improve further?

WHAT SHOULD SCHOOLS BE DOING TO PREPARE FOR AN INSPECTION?

The most important issue is that all schools should be able to out-guess Ofsted and anticipate the term when the inspection will take place. This will mean that there can be a concentration of effort in the term before a possible inspection. Much of this effort should be a series of dry runs in completing the essential paperwork that is demanded in Forms S1, S2, S3 and S4. (These are found on the disk accompanying the Ofsted Handbook.) In many ways these forms are asking you to 'tell the story' of your school in a way that shows its strengths and what has improved since the last inspection. Because the lead-in to inspections is much shorter, headteachers and governors should keep the content of the forms up to date and this should be built in to the School Development Plan. It is also important to make sure that all teachers and coordinators are well prepared. Table 9.1 suggests a wide range of areas that should be part of the process of preparation for headteachers and teachers. The cliché behind them could be that 'forewarned is at least partially forearmed'.

There will be more later in the chapter about how to prepare, manage and approach inspections with the kind of thoroughness that avoids paranoia. It is, however, worth examining the guidance provided to inspectors. In the *Primary Handbook*, p 137, paragraphs 96 and 97, there are suggestions that:

Schools should be judged primarily by their achievements, and on the effectiveness of their teaching, leadership and management in contributing to pupils' progress. Where a school is very effective, there is little need to trawl through all its procedural documents.

In the past schools have spent an inordinate amount of time in preparing policies and revising curriculum plans or schemes, largely because of a forthcoming inspection. We wish to discourage this practice.

Having read these two comments, it would be a foolish headteacher who felt that paperwork, documents, policies and schemes of work were unimportant. What it means is that in effective schools, they are perhaps *slightly less* important than they were last time.

Table 9.1 *Preparations for inspection*

It is important to spend time preparing.	Don't fall for the 'they'll have to take us as they find us' syndrome. The more that everyone knows what will happen during the inspection and the kinds of questions they will be asked, the better will be the answers they can give.
Don't leave it too late.	It's never too early to start preparing. Get an action plan, including target dates, and take responsibility for the things that you manage and coordinate. Avoid parachuting in towards an inspection with the feeling that the ground, in terms of the actual inspection date, is rushing up to meet you.
Constantly prepare for an inspection.	Everyone should work towards narrowing the gap between where the school is and where it should be. The more that planning, teaching effectively and good record keeping are a matter of routine, the less stressful an inspection visit will be.
Keep everyone informed.	Don't make the mistake of assuming that cleaners, caretakers and non-teaching staff know what an inspection entails. Tell them about it and keep them informed because everyone has a part to play in building a good impression of the school.
Avoid complacency.	If your school has had a successful inspection on a previous occasion, don't make the mistake of assuming that the next one will be equally positive. Ofsted frequently move the goal posts and the inspection team will be different.
Avoid despair.	If the last inspection was traumatic and less than good, it doesn't mean that the next one will be. If you have seriously addressed the comments made in the last inspection, there will be plenty of evidence to demonstrate the school's commitment to improve.
Put the inspection in proportion.	Don't hold long meetings every week before an inspection. It is better to have frequent short meetings with tight and specific agendas. Strong leadership will mean tackling issues systematically and making it clear to all teachers what needs to be done and said.

Documentation before an inspection

The school is in fact told what documentation is needed but there is, as has been stated previously, less time to gather the evidence. Schools will receive between six and ten weeks' notice, and in that time there should be no need for anyone to start writing and rewriting policy statements etc. In other words, there should not be a panic to produce what doesn't already exist. But, if there is a vital scheme of work which is not in place, when it is to be completed and by whom must be in the School Development Plan. A professional inspection team will want to see information that has been prepared or is in the process of being prepared as part of the 'normal' running of the school, such as the School Development Plan, subject policies and schemes of work. Most of these should be completed; in fact, realistically, all of it should be completed and be in the process of being monitored and evaluated. Ofsted suggest that they do not require any of it to be finished but only expect to see documentation that is 'normally available'. (I would hate to try to define what 'normally available' actually means.) It is important, however, to be able to demonstrate that the school is being led and managed in a way that means everyone is attempting to implement the current School Development Plan.

The inspection team

Having recognised that there are both short and long inspections, it has to be said that most schools will receive a full inspection, which will vary according to the size of the school: a small school with 4–5 classes will get 9 inspection days; a school with 301–400 children will get 26 inspection days. These inspection days will be used up over a period of a week, with the registered inspector being present for a whole week and a number of other inspectors and a lay inspector visiting for some of the days.

All teachers have the right to inspect the CVs of the inspectors in the team and all registered inspectors and their teams must abide by the code of conduct which is summarised in Table 9.2.

OBSERVING LESSONS AND TEACHING QUALITY

The inspection team will observe a sample of lessons and classes to get a cross-section of the work of the school. During the observation of lessons they will give grades for standards of achievement, the quality of learning

Table 9.2 *Inspectors' code of conduct*

All members of the inspection team are required to:

❑ be objective and impartial in evaluating the work of the school;
❑ be honest and fair in making judgements;
❑ be able to maintain integrity, courtesy and sensitivity in all dealings with staff;
❑ minimise stress, particularly by avoiding the over-inspection of individuals and by not asking for paperwork to be specially prepared for the inspection;
❑ maintain as priorities the best interests of pupils and staff;
❑ maintain a purposeful and productive dialogue with staff;
❑ respect the confidentiality of information, with particular regard for the judgements made about teachers.

and the quality of teaching. Such grades are from a three-point scale which rates:

1 as excellent or very good;
2 as good or satisfactory;
3 as less than satisfactory.

The individual profile, which every teacher receives at the end of the inspection, indicates which grade the observed lessons were given. For the purposes of the final inspection report, a calculation is made of the percentage of lessons that were satisfactory or better or the percentage that were less than satisfactory. In addition, a confidential report is made to the headteacher listing teachers and their grades so that he or she can decide what use to make of them. No such naming of teachers will be made in the final report, but the clear implication is that the headteacher should begin to take action as soon as the inspectors have left.

The inspection team are also required to offer oral feedback to individual teachers on the quality of teaching seen. This is supposed to take place either at the end of the lesson or as soon as possible afterwards. It is not compulsory to receive this feedback but teachers should be given the opportunity to explain the context of any difficulties they may have encountered during the lesson.

It is lesson observation and the grading of quality that causes the most stress and yet, in a way, can be planned for and managed by a high-quality senior management team and in schools where the concept of working together is well established. Troman and Woods (2001) in *Primary Teachers' Stress* suggested that as a result of a negative Ofsted report, 'They [teachers] experienced feelings of guilt, shame and self doubt and felt themselves to be inadequate, fraudulent and stigmatised. The grading of teachers led to divisiveness among them' (2001: 134). They go on to say in even more blunt terms:

> It is now clear that policies of naming, blaming and shaming and the management styles and systems of Ofsted are increasingly out of step with new management approaches being introduced. . . where the 'softer' styles are increasingly becoming established. . . . It is unlikely that Ofsted style inspections which have damaged teachers. . . and have a questionable relationship in raising the quality of education will be replaced with the type of 'no blame' inspections advocated by some in the USA and in the UK (2001: 138).

Preparing for classroom observation

No school wants to fail and no teacher wants to be thought of as less than satisfactory, and what is more, no headteacher wants his or her school and teachers to be thought of as underperforming. It is important to have a system in place where classes are observed regularly. This can be both part of the performance management cycle and also part of how the school is managed to improve the quality of teaching. In Chapter 7 there was a long section on 'monitoring the quality of teaching' and it is important to make sure that when it is done it is done properly with agreed pro formas, an agreed focus and time after the observation for informed feedback which emphasises targets for improvement. If this is not part of a school's ethos and there are concerns that introducing a system of observation and feedback will damage the school's fragile structure, then one way of starting it is for headteachers to observe alongside an LEA inspector in a series of planned paired observations. This also should not be limited to the headteacher. Subject coordinators also have to be trained to observe lessons and manage the quality of teaching in their subject.

Judging teachers

Headteachers and coordinators need to know as much about the quality of teaching as possible and how they know it is because they have observed lessons and found out what is happening in classrooms. Headteachers need to know how they feel about quality before Ofsted arrive ready to name and shame those whom they perceive as inadequate. If your school has a weak teacher, what are you doing about it? You need to know because Ofsted will certainly ask you.

Let's go over some of the areas that Ofsted will be thoroughly delving into. After all, the more you know about the enemy, the easier it is to plan the battle and win it.

Inspectors must evaluate and report on the quality of teaching judged in terms of its impact on children's learning and what makes it successful or not. They must evaluate:

❏ how well the skills of literacy and numeracy are taught;
❏ how well the school meets the needs of all its pupils, taking into account age, gender, ethnicity, SEN, able children and those who have English as a second language;
❏ the teaching in each subject, commenting on variations between subjects and year groups.

Every headteacher, deputy, senior teacher, subject coordinator and class teacher should be able to ask themselves similar questions related to their school and their classroom, such as:

❏ How well is literacy taught across the school/key stage?
❏ How well is numeracy taught in Mrs X's classroom?
❏ How do we meet the needs of SEN children?
❏ How well does Mr Y meet the needs of his SEN children in his classroom?
❏ Do we take ethnicity into account? If we do, how does it manifest itself?

As part of the planning for an Ofsted inspection it is possible to convert what Ofsted is looking for into questions that schools and teachers can ask of themselves. I won't do it again, because it is so obvious. Figure 9.3 lists a whole variety of issues that Ofsted will consider when making their judgements. An effective school will already have considered them before Ofsted arrive and will be doing something about any areas of weakness that they found in their pre-Ofsted audit of their own good practice.

Many of these areas of teaching and learning have been discussed in Chapter 7 in more detail but, as you can imagine, there are some important pre-inspection questions to be asked.

How good are curricular opportunities

The inspection team that arrives in your school one Monday morning has to report on:

Table 9.3 *Judging teachers*

In reaching their judgements Ofsted will consider whether teachers:	The inspection team will also examine the extent to which children:
❏ have a good knowledge of their subject and are able to show understanding by the way they present it to their children;	❏ acquire new knowledge or skills, develop ideas and increase their understanding;
❏ are technically competent in teaching phonics and other basic skills;	❏ apply themselves to their work, intellectually, physically and creatively;
❏ plan effectively and are able to set clear objectives that their children understand;	❏ are productive, work at a good pace and show interest in their work;
❏ challenge and inspire children by expecting the most out of them and by deepening their knowledge and understanding;	❏ can sustain concentration and think and learn for themselves;
❏ use teaching methods so that all children learn effectively;	❏ understand what they are doing, how well they have done and how they can improve.
❏ manage children well and expect high standards of behaviour;	
❏ use resources such as time, teaching assistants and ICT effectively;	
❏ assess children's work thoroughly and use any assessments to help overcome difficulties;	
❏ use homework to reinforce and/or extend what is learnt in school.	

❏ the quality and range of learning opportunities, which includes identifying strengths and weaknesses of extra curricular support, PSHE and links with the community;

❏ whether the school meets statutory requirements including Religious Education;

❑ how well the school develops the children's personal, spiritual, moral, social and cultural development.

These broad issues will mean that each coordinator has to ask some equally broad questions that fit into the subject that they are responsible for. For example:

❑ Are the range of learning opportunities adequate in your subject?
❑ What are the strengths and weaknesses of extra curricular activities?
❑ How can you show that children's personal, spiritual, moral, social and cultural development is actually being 'developed'? What actually happens?

SELF-AUDITING HOW WELL PUPILS ARE TAUGHT

This has been said before and needs to be repeated again and again: Ofsted inspectors will come into your school with their own preconceived ideas about what the school is like. They will have got their information about the school from the last inspection report, the school's latest PANDA and other statistical data such as absences and unauthorised absences.

The headteacher and all the teachers need to know more about the school and its successes and reasons for its success than the inspectors. It is vitally important to be able to tell the inspectors how teachers teach, for example, and how effective you think the curriculum actually is.

Providing evidence that you and your coordinators have been monitoring teaching quality should be easy because there should be a system of doing this in place. The fact that you have been monitoring the quality of teaching will mean that you will have been able to make your own judgements on whether children are learning as much, as quickly, and progressing as well as you would expect.

When making judgements about the quality of teaching, you will need to bear in mind the following, which are summarised from *Inspecting Schools: Handbook for Inspecting Primary and Nursery Schools* (Ofsted, 1999) and which are discussed in more detail in Smith (2000) *Meeting the Challenges of Curriculum 2000*:

❑ If almost all the teaching is good or better, with no unsatisfactory teaching, then the overall quality could be judged as good.
❑ The overall quality of teaching is unsatisfactory if more than 1 in 10 lessons are judged as unsatisfactory, ie 10 per cent of all lessons. (This means that 90 per cent of all lessons have to be satisfactory or better!)

❏ If these unsatisfactory lessons are judged to be poor or very poor and this proportion is seen to be higher than 1 in 8, ie 12 per cent, then the phrase 'serious weakness' will be considered.

❏ Once the proportion of unsatisfactory teaching reaches 1 lesson out of 5, ie 20 per cent, your school is likely to be classed by Ofsted as in need of special measures.

The above points suggest very strongly that your and your coordinator's observations of lessons needs to be completed within a consistent framework of what is quality teaching. Ofsted's characteristics are summarised in Table 9.4 and include:

❏ very good or excellent lessons;
❏ those that are satisfactory or better;
❏ lessons that are unsatisfactory or worse.

SELF-AUDITING CURRICULAR OPPORTUNITIES

The first thing to do before Ofsted look at a wide range of evidence to evaluate your school's curriculum provision is to make sure that your school meets the DfEE's recommendation for taught time in each key stage. (Chapter 8 has examples of breakdowns of curriculum time from Key Stage 1, Infants and Key Stage 2, Juniors.) The inspectors will also look for evidence that the school and each subject has clear statements about the curriculum, including what is said in the broadest terms in the school prospectus. The inspectors will collect evidence about whether the curriculum meets statutory requirements as well as how well it provides for the spiritual, moral, social and cultural development of all children. In Table 9.5 there are other characteristics that will help you in your audit.

AT THE END OF THE INSPECTION WEEK

When the inspectors begin feeding back verbally what will actually be in their report, it is important to take detailed notes. The accuracy of the inspectors' information can be corrected but their judgements cannot.

Verbal feedback is given to subject coordinators in the presence of the head or a senior teacher and this information should be fed back to colleagues. A verbal report is given to the headteacher and other invited

Table 9.4 *Characteristics of the quality of lessons*

VERY GOOD OR EXCELLENT LESSONS	LESSONS THAT ARE SATISFACTORY OR BETTER	LESSONS THAT ARE UNSATISFACTORY OR WORSE
❏ The teacher is knowledgeable, stimulating and perceptive.	❏ The teaching of basic skills and the subject content is clear and accurate.	❏ Knowledge of the subject being taught is insufficient to promote demanding work.
❏ The teacher uses imaginative resources and makes intellectual and creative demands on children that extend their learning.	❏ There are clear explanations and demonstrations involving all children.	❏ Basic skills are not taught effectively.
❏ Challenging questions are used that consolidate, extend and verify what children know and understand.	❏ Lesson organisation allows most children to keep up with the work and complete it in the available time.	❏ Many children are not engaged in the lesson.
❏ The teaching methods match the demands of the lesson and make the best use of the time available.	❏ Teacher–child interaction checks understanding.	❏ Lessons are poorly planned.
❏ There is a confident, positive atmosphere where children can achieve.	❏ Most children are on task for most of the time.	❏ Lessons are not organised well and teaching time is wasted.
❏ Children are keen to rise to challenges and are thoughtful.	❏ Teacher–child relationships mean that children do their work and understand how well they have done.	❏ Classroom discipline is weak.
❏ Children work well and make progress.		❏ Children do not know what they are doing in the lesson.
		❏ Children are not making sufficient progress.

members of staff. In primary schools, I would suggest that the whole staff attend this meeting and challenge the views of the inspectors and ask as many questions for clarification as necessary. It is important not to let the inspector set too short a time span for this meeting. It needs to last as long as necessary to get as much information as possible on how judgements were reached and it is probably advisable to make sure that a reasonable

Table 9.5 *Curriculum characteristics*

A VERY GOOD OR BETTER CURRICULUM	A SATISFACTORY OR BETTER CURRICULUM	A CURRICULUM THAT IS UNSATISFACTORY OR WORSE
❑ The statutory requirements are interpreted in ways that are stimulating as well as structured.	❑ The curriculum meets the statutory requirements and takes into account the literacy and numeracy strategies.	❑ Statutory requirements, including significant aspects of the core subjects, are not met.
❑ It provides for a wide range of abilities including high achievement.	❑ There will be some additional activities provided for children of different ages and needs.	❑ There is too little account made of the literacy and numeracy strategies.
❑ Additional opportunities are offered over and above the core subjects.	❑ There will be a reasonable use of resources within the wider community, including visits that contribute to children's learning.	❑ The children do not understand respect or tolerance.
❑ A high priority is given to developing basic skills.		❑ Their standard of behaviour is poor.
❑ Resources from both within and outside the school are used to enrich the curriculum.	❑ Some children are able to exercise responsibility and initiative.	❑ There are also few opportunities for personal development and cultural enrichment.
❑ Children are given opportunities to develop personal initiative and responsibility.	❑ Most children understand the difference between right and wrong.	
❑ They clearly understand the difference between right and wrong.	❑ Most children are able to respect the traditions, values and beliefs of others.	
❑ Children have a high degree of respect for the differences between people's values and beliefs.		
❑ The curriculum shows evidence of drawing positively on pupils' cultural, family and religious backgrounds.		

amount of time is available for the inspectors to report their findings to the governors.

A summary report is then produced which must be sent to all parents and there is a full report which does not have to be sent to the parents but which must be made available if they want to read it, or want their own copy.

The next stage is to produce a carefully worded press report which highlights all the positive things that the inspectors said about the school. Obviously, if there were some less than flattering aspects in a generally positive report, it is important to make sure that the press report refers to it but avoids highlighting it. Most local papers seem to be run on the maxim that 'the only good news is bad news' and, while they do genuinely write articles on good Ofsted reports in local newspapers, I have the feeling that they leap with joy if they can get their hands on a poor one.

The final stage, if the report is a reasonably good one, is to prepare the action plan, which, when it is completed, has to be sent to all parents, the Ofsted team and the LEA. This is what the school intends to do and the action it intends taking on the priorities which the inspectors highlighted in their key issues. Each action plan is different because in each school the key issues will be different, but it must list the issues for action and their order of importance in raising standards. What this means is that the inspectors will identify weaknesses and the school plans to take action in order to change the weaknesses to strengths.

It might be the case that the action plan will contain issues that have already been identified in the school's own action plan. If this happens then the task ahead is much simpler, although the completion times might need to be looked at with a certain amount of urgency. If Ofsted have found areas that were not in the development plan, or there are issues that they have recognised as more important than you have, then the development plan needs to be changed to absorb any new issues. In my opinion the post-Ofsted Action Plan needs to exist as a separate document for at least two years before it is totally absorbed into the development planning process. It is simplistic but true that a school with a reasonable or better Inspection report will be quite capable of producing and acting on a post-inspection plan. Unfortunately, some schools are not so lucky.

UNDER-PERFORMING SCHOOLS

For the substantial majority of schools the outcome of an inspection is a report that is largely complimentary, with some key issues to tackle over

Table 9.6 *Factors relating to serious weaknesses*

A school is considered to have serious weaknesses when one or more of the following factors are present:

❏ Standards are unsatisfactory in four or more subjects across the school as a whole, or in particular key stages. Particular attention is given to unsatisfactory standards in English, Maths and Science.
❏ The quality of teaching and learning is unsatisfactory in more than approximately 1 in 8 lessons.
❏ There are concerns about the standards of the children's behaviour and conduct or about relationships generally.
❏ The management is ineffective.
❏ The school does not give value for money.
❏ The level of attendance is below 90%.
❏ There are more than five exclusions in any one year.

the next year or two. Occasionally, the performance of a school is judged to be unsatisfactory. If a school is likely to fail to give a satisfactory standard of education to its children then it could be put into the category of having 'serious weaknesses' or at worst become subject to 'special measures'. It is these two categories that all headteachers need to be concerned about. Table 9.6 lists some of the criteria used by the inspectors for making judgements about the failings of a school.

If the registered inspector thinks that the school may have very 'serious weaknesses' then it may become subject to 'special measures'. S/he will inform the headteacher and contact Ofsted's Schools at Risk Team (SART). Within three weeks HMI visit the school to check on aspects of the Inspector's report and if they agree that the school is failing, then the school is confirmed as subject to Special Measures. This will then involve six monthly follow up visits from HMI to see if the school is implementing its action plan and if this is likely to eliminate the school's weaknesses.

There is now another category of 'failure' in Ofsted's armoury to raise standards. Inspectors may judge that your school is 'underachieving'. They are likely to reach this judgement if the school has not raised standards at a similar rate to other schools when looked at over time and not just in comparison with the previous year. Apparently, this would not be the case automatically because standards in some schools are already high. In other schools standards may fall because the nature of the intake may change significantly. It is not clear what happens to schools that are judged to be 'underachieving'. It is expected that HMI will monitor those schools in some way and Ofsted may decide to inspect such schools again after two years.

STRATEGIES FOR SURVIVING AN OFSTED INSPECTION

It is obvious that managing a school that has serious weaknesses or is classed as underachieving would be extremely difficult. Questions would be asked about all aspects of the school but the culture of 'blame' would fall heavily on the quality of teaching and the quality of leadership. It would be difficult to retain the staff, difficult to retrain those who remained in post and probably impossible to maintain morale and minimise stress.

Self-evaluation

Self-audits and self-evaluation, and this has already been raised earlier in the chapter, should help schools to find out what their weaknesses are before an inspection and with hard work do something about it before the inspectors arrive. In fact, Ofsted have raised their own expectations about the extent to which schools employ self-evaluation procedures. One theme running through the new framework is for inspectors to evaluate the rigour with which schools evaluate their own performance. The questions raised are not just 'what do you know about your own school?' but 'how effectively do you find out?' This has significant implications for governors because they are advised to revisit their understanding of and methods by which they undertake their roles of establishing a strategic direction, ensuring accountability and acting as critical friend.

Documentation

Important documentation should be in place before an inspection. No one should be required to create documentation, although there is no reason why existing policies and schemes of work should not be re-edited and tidied up for the inspectors to see.

It is important to make sure that you are implementing the School Development Plan. And it is no good having other policies in place unless everyone is working to them rather than ignoring them.

The School Development Plan should already have prioritised key issues as well as completion dates for all the tasks that have been identified. For those areas that you have not addressed, show that you plan to do them in the future. Don't ever suggest that you will never attempt something (even if you think it is a mixture of a waste of time, impracticable, unworkable etc), because they may argue that you are:

❑   not meeting statutory requirements;
❑   not giving children full access to the National Curriculum;
❑   neglecting your responsibilities.

If everyone is fully briefed and they can anticipate the criticism and prepare any responses in advance, then it may be possible to avoid some of the critical points that otherwise might have appeared as an action point on the completed report.

Work together as a whole school team

The most important and key point to make here is NEVER use an Ofsted inspection or any meeting with an inspector as an opportunity to get any grievances off your chest or to gripe about how badly managed the school is, how Mrs X never shares resources, how difficult it is to get the young teachers to hand in their planning on time etc. Don't moan, because if you do, you will be giving the inspectors ammunition with which to shoot you down. Work closely as a team, emphasise teamwork and convince them that the school is a harmonious place full of hard-working and committed teachers and children. This will help you to get a report that will be as positive as possible and will not leave you with much work to do after the inspectors have left.

MAKING THE INSPECTION AS POSITIVE AN EXPERIENCE AS POSSIBLE!

The best I can say is that an Ofsted inspection is a supposedly important way of helping schools recognise their own strengths and weaknesses. At its worst, it is four days of major disruption resulting in most cases in a report that tells you what you already know in language that has a much more negative flow than it does positive. In the spring of 2000, Ofstin (The Office for Standards in Inspection) brought out a report, *The Ofsted System of School Inspection: An Independent Evaluation*. Some of their findings included here are important because they will help all schools put their individual experiences, unfortunately more negative than positive, within a wider and larger context:

❑   Many schools perceived the inspection system as punitive and threatening.

❑ Many teachers feel unable to speak out publicly about their experiences even though these may have been traumatic, leaving deep scars and a real sense of injustice.

❑ They do not speak out because they fear the potential consequences to themselves or their schools of being identified.

❑ These numbers may not be great but the fact that the inspection can and does generate such fear and apprehension is a serious criticism of government in a democratic system.

❑ There is real concern that the Ofsted system of inspection is moving schools towards a rigid culture decided and imposed from without.

❑ The acceptance of an imposed culture leads to a closed situation in which a higher value is placed on obedience and implementation than on critical thinking, innovation and professional dialogue; yet the latter are the essential ingredients of an improvement culture.

❑ The present inspection regime is in great danger of replacing the open learning dynamic of schools with an autocratic unquestioned orthodoxy.

❑ The summative, judgemental outcomes of inspection are not effective in promoting reflective professional development within schools.

❑ Ofsted's approach must change from the adversarial to the collaborative.

❑ There must be a continuous link, in one form or another, between inspectors and the school, based on an interchange of advice and assistance arising from the inspection.

Schools, at the moment, have to live within the boundaries of the Ofsted system of inspection. In an effective school, there will be a vision which will be at the heart of the curriculum and of teaching. Inspectors will, despite the negative comments about the whole of the Ofsted process, be looking for these 'visions' and, more than that, will be looking for their translation into practice. Good management will ensure that they will see whole curriculum planning as a reality, where all the teachers appreciate the necessity of high-quality teaching of a broad and balanced curriculum.

IMPORTANT POINTS

It seems to me that the key to managing an Ofsted inspection is to know more about your school than they do and to be able to 'tell the story' of your school to a registered inspector in a way that will neutralise any issues that the inspector will have on his or her agenda from the bare statistics that are available about the school and before he or she even walks through the school door:

❏ Before the inspection, audit your school and evaluate the quality of the teaching and the quality of what is taught.

❏ Make sure that documentation such as the School Development Plan and subject policy statements are in place and are being acted upon.

❏ Understand what the inspection team will do during their days in school.

❏ It is important to understand the Ofsted criteria for success and failure.

❏ Audit the strengths of the teaching in such a way that you and the subject coordinators are aware of any individual's strengths and weaknesses.

❏ Make sure that all teachers understand the kinds of judgements that will be made in the final report, which is, of course, a public document.

❏ Emphasise to all staff the need to work together, to maintain the strength of teams and never to say anything negative to an inspector.

CONCLUSION

This is not an attempt to summarise the book or to pick out more key points from each chapter. It is, however, an attempt to return to the complex issue of leadership which is one of the key elements of the Introduction and of Chapter 6. There is still no brilliant definition that will bring clarity to a difficult subject and yet it is still accepted that without effective leadership schools cannot raise standards. Schools do need the sense of direction provided by strong leadership and this will come from the headteacher who will be the key leader, with all the skills that this means. Leithwood *et al* (1999), in *Changing Leadership for Changing Times*, take the concept of leadership a stage further: '. . . we are coming to believe that leaders are those people who "walk ahead", people who are genuinely committed to deep change in themselves and in their organisations. They lead through developing new skills, capabilities and understandings. *And they come from many places within the organisations.*' (1999: 85) [my italics]

They have introduced the idea that there are many leaders in the school and I have stressed that all curriculum coordinators must be both allowed to lead and able to lead. In the Introduction, Table 0.1, there were distinctions drawn between 'management' and 'leadership' and there is no doubt in my mind that the headteacher and any other designated subject leader has to be able to 'manage'. They have to be able to solve problems, for example, maintain the status quo, plan, organise and control, and set up systems and structures that work and keep the school running smoothly and effectively. Leadership, however, is about those personal qualities that make it possible to manage successfully and sustain high performance of oneself and others. I am going to close the book with some definitions of personal and social competence that will determine how we manage ourselves, how we lead and manage colleagues and how we learn from colleagues and are able to support them in maintaining their own successes. We need to end positively and avoid the Ofsted syndrome where, if there had been a registered inspector around in Galilee in 32 AD he or she would have taken Jesus aside after he had walked on water and asked him when he was going to learn to swim.

How do we manage and lead ourselves?

❑ Recognise our own emotions and their effect on other people.
❑ Know one's own strengths and weaknesses.
❑ Have a strong sense of one's own self-worth and capabilities.
❑ Be able to keep disruptive emotions and impulses in check.
❑ Maintain high standards of honesty and integrity.
❑ Take responsibility for one's own personal performance.
❑ Be able to be flexible in handling change.
❑ Be comfortable with new ideas, the development of new approaches and new information.
❑ Keep striving to be good at the job.
❑ Be ready to act and develop new opportunities.
❑ Be persistent in pursuing goals despite obstacles and setbacks.

How do we manage to lead others?

❑ There is a need to 'sense' colleagues' feelings and to know when to act and when to draw back.
❑ Colleagues have to have their development needs recognised.
❑ Anticipate, recognise and meet the needs of colleagues within the framework of the school's development needs.
❑ Cultivate opportunities to make changes and develop areas through colleagues.
❑ Know what tactics will be effective for 'persuading' colleagues to complete tasks.
❑ Listen and send convincing messages.
❑ Inspire and guide individuals and groups.
❑ Work with others towards shared goals.

And finally, although Ofsted do not attempt to define what good, effective and successful leadership is (if they did, we could all aspire to it), they do suggest the following in the *Handbook for Inspecting Primary and Nursery Schools* (Ofsted, 1999): Leadership is concerned with (and this must be a large part of a headteacher's job):

❑ creating and securing commitment to a clear vision;
❑ managing change so as to improve the school;
❑ building a high-performing team;
❑ inspiring, motivating and influencing staff;
❑ leading by example and taking responsibility.

So. . . as you always imagined, a relatively easy job!

REFERENCES

Bell, D (1992) Co-ordinating science in the primary school: a role model, *Evaluation and Research in Education*, **6** (2–3), pp 155–71

Bell, L (1989) *Management Skills in Primary Schools*, Routledge, London

Brand, T (1993) The first week and how to survive it, *Child Education*, Scholastic, Leamington Spa

Clemson, D (1996) Informal technology in the national curriculum, in *The Primary Core National Curriculum: Policy into Practice*, ed D Coulby and S Ward, Cassell, London

Day, C, Whittaker, P and Johnston, D (1990) *Managing Primary Schools in the 1990's: A Professional Development Approach*, Paul Chapman, London

Dean, J (1987) *Managing the Primary School*, Routledge, London

DES (1991) *Development Planning: a Practical Guide*, HMSO, London

DES (1990) *Developing School Management: The Way Forward*, HMSO, London

DfEE (1993) *Curriculum Organisation and Classroom Practice: A Follow up Report*, The Stationery Office, Norwich

DfEE (1998) *Teachers: Meeting the Challenge of Change*, HMSO, London

DfEE (1999) *The National Curriculum Handbook*, HMSO, London

DfEE (2000) *Threshold Assessment: Guidance on Completing the Application*, HMSO, London

Elliott, H and Kemp, J (1983) The management of stress: figure and ground, *Educational Change and Development*, **7** (2), pp 19–23

Elton Report (1989) *Discipline in Schools: Report of the Committee of Enquiry Chaired by Lord Elton*, HMSO, London

Everard, K B (1986) *Developing Management in Schools*, Blackwell, Oxford

Everard, K B and Morris, G (1985) *Effective School Management*, Harper and Row, London

Gadsby, P and Harrison, M (1999) *The Primary Coordinator and Ofsted Reinspection*, Falmer, London

Hand, G (1981) First call on your adviser: the INSET role of advisers, in *Inservice the Teacher and the School*, ed C Donoughue (1982), Kogan Page, London

Handy, C (1976) *Understanding Organisations*, Penguin, London

Harrison, M A and Gill, S C (1992) *Primary School Management*, Heinemann, London

HMI (1977) *Ten Good Schools*, HMSO, London

Leithwood, K, Jantzi, D and Steinbach, R (1999) *Changing Leadership for Changing Times*, University of Toronto, Canada

Lewin, K (1947) *Human relations*, University of Chicago Press, Chicago

Montgomery, D (1989) *Managing Behaviour Problems*, Hodder and Stoughton, London

Mortimore, P, Sammons, P, Stoll, L, Lewis, D and Ecob, R (1988) *School Matters: The Junior Years*, Open Books, London

Ofsted (1999) *Inspecting Schools: Handbook for Inspecting Primary and Nursery Schools*, HMSO, London

Ofstin (2000) *The Ofsted System of School Inspection: An Independent Evaluation*, A Report by the Centre for the Evaluation of Public Policy and Practice and the Helix Consulting Group, Ofstin, Northumberland

Pedlar, M (1986) *A Manager's Guide to Self Development*, Hodder and Stoughton, London

Playfoot, D, Skelton, M and Southworth, G (1989) *The Primary School Management Book*, Mary Glasgow Publications, London

Rogers, C (1980) *A Way of Being*, Houghton Mifflin, Boston

Rowland, V and Birkett, K (1992) *Personal Effectiveness for Teachers*, Simon and Schuster, London

Rutter, M, Maughan B, Mortimore, P, Ouston, J and Smith, A (1979) *Fifteen Thousand Hours: Secondary Schools and Their Effects on Children*, Open Books, London

SCAA (1999) *Teaching for Effective Learning: A Paper for Discussion and Development*, SCAA, London

Smith, R (1993) *Preparing for Appraisal: Self Evaluation for Teachers in Primary and Secondary Schools*, Framework Press, Lancaster

Smith, R (1995) *Successful School Management*, Cassell, London

Smith, R (2000) *Performance Management and Threshold Assessment, Packs 1 and 2*, Pearson Publishing, Cambridge

Smith, R (2000) *Raising Achievement in the Primary School*, Pearson Publishing, Cambridge

Smith, R (2001) *Making Your School More Successful: Packs 1 and 2*, Pearson Publishing, Cambridge

Troman, G and Woods, P (2001) *Primary Teachers' Stress*, Routledge–Falmer, London

TTA (1998) *National Standards for Subject Leaders*, Teacher Training Agency, London

WCC (1998) *The Plan is the School*, Warwickshire County Council, Warwick

INDEX